48 RULES FOR RAGING AGAINST THE WORLD

How To Use Unorthodox Morals To Recognize & Fight Corrupt Behavior

By James S. Zakaria

Dedicated to my family and the thought leaders who have influenced me the most

The Courageous James Altucher, the Articulate Jordan Peterson, the Adventurous Mark Manson, the Charming Jay Shetty, the Eloquent Robin Sharma, the Daring Brene Brown, the Wise Depak Chopra, the Admirable Malcolm Gladwell, the Hilarious Jen Sincero, the Original Seth Godin, the Agreeable Lewis Howes, the Genuine Don Miguel Ruiz, the Dynamic Patrick Bet-David, the Compassionate Marie Forleo, the Conscientious Vishen Lakhiani, the Impressive Ryan Holiday, the Brilliant Robert Greene, the Passionate Eric Thomas, the Insightful Gary John Bishop, the Captivating Elizabeth Gilbert, the Extraordinary Tony Robbins, and the Charismatic Tom Bilyeu

Contents

1. INTRODUCTION

Maybe he should kill himself off? This thought entered the mind of the driver as he raced through the city streets. Which means of suicide would be the least bloody and painful to him and his family? Probably prescription pills. Toss some in his mouth, and he would never wake up. All his problems would evaporate like the wind.

He shook his head and wondered where such awful ideas originated. He was not the type. Maybe the last few months had been kind of depressing, but it was the dead of winter after all. Nah, what a stupid….

A more booming voice resonated within. "You ponder throwing away your life because there is no greater purpose, no reason for being, no direction for growth. Working, spending & waiting for retirement is not a comprehensive plan that satisfies. A weak set of values, morals, & principles, driving you to build a family, career, business, or community project is not enough to bring you home."

The first sound that interrupted his thoughts was the screech of tires grinding against brake pads. The sound of shattering glass and crunching bumpers filled Will's ears as he slammed his right foot on his car brake as hard he could. His head whipped forward and then back like a cheap marionette doll on a string; his vision overflowed with stars and bright lights. Had he smashed the Audi in front with his

BMW? He could hear the rumble of a thousand honeybees and then dead silence.

Will realized that his car had just missed hitting the car in front of him by inches. The Audi sedan driver crashed into the Ford pickup one car length ahead of him. None of the other drivers seemed injured thanks to their seatbelts and airbags. That was a relief. After carefully examining his vehicle for scratches and giving a statement to the police officers who arrived at the scene, Will got back in the driver's seat.

He thought about how silly his thoughts were. One moment he was thinking about destroying a precious life, the next, he was angrily protecting a silver conveyance of German engineering and design. He would put more stock into an object of metal, glass, plastic, and wires than his soul's existence? He shook his head at the madness of it all.

2. Moral Philosophy - Seize Your Destiny By Avoiding The Dark Side

Will was sitting at a table at an old fashioned diner restaurant six blocks from his apartment when he walked in and sat down at the table next to him. He was an older adult wearing a long grey winter coat covering a dark suit and polished dress shoes, mired with mud & sleet in his sixties.

Looking him over, the man had both the dark coloring of an African and the physical features of a person from Japan. This combination caught Will's attention; he assumed the senior was mixed-race and wondered about his family history.

The customer had frizzy greying hair, dark circles under his eyes, and age spots on his skin but seemed to have more energy and vitality than the pair of twenty something men at the other end of the room.

"Hey, can I borrow the sports section, please?" the man asked.

Will handed it over to him and continued to read the news section of the local newspaper.

"Thank you. Just checking the scores. My friends call me Morgan."

"Hi, I am Will. Will Evans.

"What do you do? For a living?"

"I am a senior civil engineer at Magnatecx Consulting. How about you?"

"Well, retired, of course."

"Cool," Will replied.

"You seem like a bright fellow. An engineer, of course. But it appears to me that you are kind of a philosopher at heart. Someone who thinks about heady concepts: life, birth, life, morality, and death. Am I right?"

"Sometimes, while I am in the shower or driving, I might think about those things from time to time," Will admitted.

"At my age, I had years to study the topic, read many books, think about it, and I have figured out one immutable truth."

"What is that?" he asked.

"It occurred to me while assembling a do-it-yourself wood cabinet. I didn't quite understand the confusing instruction manual and struggled to put all the pieces in place. Some I put in backward, and other parts had no place to put them in. Instead of being a one hour job, the poorly written booklet helped turn the project into a four-hour ordeal."

Will waited, intrigued.

"Everyone I have ever met is facing the same existential struggle. Other people are also trying to build a life, working off their own incomplete owners' instructional manual. Each of us is attempting to grow up, start a career, get married, and have children using grossly incomplete instructional booklets. All of our owner's manuals, or Lifebooks, are missing pages, have blank spaces, and it is up to us to replace the old rules of conduct that worked for our parents but no longer succeed for us[i]."

"That is a unique way of putting it," Will acknowledged.

"Here is where it gets complicated. There is no one universal owner's manual that applies to everyone. We all have to build our version, unique to our circumstances. It takes a lifetime to complete because aging changes our circumstances in ways that require new instructions for each stage of life."

"For some people figuring out their lives is very difficult. They had absent or negligent parents. Maybe they were born into a life of crime and poverty. There was no place or resources for them to get help, so they had to figure out themselves. Very difficult to win under those conditions."

"Other children are blessed with loving parents who taught them right from wrong. They had good schooling, supportive friends, and self-confidence in themselves. Their owner's manual was thick with ideas and filled with lessons, so becoming a successful adult was a matter of executing what they learned and finding those missing pieces."

Will asked, "So, you believe that our fate and circumstances control our lives?"

"Not at all. We all are capable of building the life we think we deserve. Anyone, of any color, gender, or creed, can construct a magnificent Lifebook if they want to put effort into it. It is just that life can be cruel and unkind to some, so they start on their journey with a few fuzzy lines on a piece of paper."

"Others win life's lottery, and they build a solid Lifebook filled with thousands of pages on how to talk to strangers, finish projects, make friends, find quality partners, and persuade and win the hearts of the public. Nobody said life is fair, but we must deal with the hands we're given."

"Do you teach people how to be successful?" Will asked.

"Ha, ha, ha. Sorry, I laughed. Success is a very nebulous word that means so many things to so many people. You might already be successful and not realize it. Or your high standards sabotage your efforts to reach your goals? Maybe the success you desire will be easy to achieve, and it's as simple as pushing the start button. No, teaching success is a topic of expertise that I am not inclined to participate in."

"My concern is about what kind of society we are building as people thrash about and bump into each other while they try to figure out what class of Lifebook they want to create for themselves. Far too many are ignoring the common good in favor of money-making, and we are trading our spiritual wealth for a mechanistic-militaristic sociopathic form of capitalism."

Will was confused, "People are thrashing and bumping? What does that mean?"

"Perfect question. Every nasty, negative, and mean character you encounter does not really want to be that way. People struggle to make sense of their world and sometimes make unpleasant comments, are abrupt, or say unthoughtful ideas because they don't know better. That's what I call thrashing & failing. They would rather not do these things but don't have alternative answers."

"Man, you want us to have compassion for these people? After all the nasty stuff they do to us?" Will disliked that idea.

"When you have empathy for others, you build up self-compassion for yourself. Be nice, Will, so you can have a kind soul to share with others."

Morgan took a sip of coffee while Will thought about this philosophy. Maybe he should be more agreeable to others if they are just as lost and confused.

"I hope I am not boring you. Some people don't like preachers of philosophy. They get offended when you point out other ways of being."

"No, that is fine. This topic is quite fascinating," Will said.

"Most people act without really thinking about the consequences. They do things that are self-destructive or based on the desires of others. Most are wildly out of control because their emotions are in charge. Folks are pulled into their lives, making decisions from forces they don't recognize or control[ii]."

"You look confused, so let me appropriate this tale from another teacher:"

"An old Cherokee grandfather is telling his grandson a story. 'A fight is going on inside me," he said. "It is a terrible fight between two wolves. One is evil - he is anger, envy, greed, arrogance, resentment, and lies.'"

Morgan continued, "the other is good - he is joy, peace, love, hope, humility, kindness, generosity, truth, and faith. The wolves are battling to the death."

"Enthralled, the boy asks his grandfather which wolf will win. The old Cherokee simply replied 'the one you feed the most.'"

Will gave his praise, "That is a great story."

"Yes. Each of us has competing wolves, spirits, or sides to fight to build the person we are to become. **If we let the dark wolf take over, our Lifebook will begin to fill with pages of anger, sadness, fear, and regret. If we act in a way that feeds our light wolf, our owners' manuals fill up**

with pages of happiness, generosity, courage, and strength."

Will asked, "And that can make us healthy, wealthy, and successful?"

"You certainly will have the energy and positivity to go after your dreams with gusto and vigor."

"Nothing is as simple as we would like it to be. Humans don't understand themselves at all. They can feel the wolves raging in themselves but not see it happening to others. It is challenging to observe that bad people can do helpful things, and nice people can do immoral things as well[iii]."

"Once people judge negative attributes or positive characteristics in a person, most label them as either purely good or bad. With this error in judgment, people welcome those they perceive as safe and shun those who are dangerous to their values."

"This 'all or nothing' type of thinking is very destructive to the thinker and those in their community. Can you see both sides of an argument and see either as equally valid? Will? Can you be objective and rational when most people are not?"

"Logical thinking is key to being consistent in your actions; otherwise, you will unconsciously act kindly to some and be harsh with others."

"I believe so. I have gone back and forth on the rightness of certain actions," Will stated his position.

"No rational person wants to be seen as a bad person. They don't mind being a rule breaker but being a morally despicable criminal is too much to handle. So he or she hides or represses all his or her awful thoughts and sins away[iv]. Pretends that it never happened. Lies and deceives if confronted. This mental blockage creates a blind spot in people and prevents them from taking the right actions."

Will said, "Can I recap this? The dark wolf in us makes us do bad things. We pretend it didn't happen because we can't cope with our mistakes. Then we build a Lifebook built on delusions and lies?"

"Yes, yes, yes. Will, you are a worthy student. Exactly."

"One correction. You are always in charge of your actions. You feed both the white wolf and the dark wolf. You become the wolf you choose to feed."

"Ah," the engineer said.

"Before I utter anything else, I would like a promise that you don't share this knowledge with anyone who can't tolerate subversive & liberal ideas that contradict their worldview. That means don't antagonize conservatives or liberals, capitalists or socialists, or any person of faith by telling them they could be making numerous errors in judgment or arguing with them about politics. Promise?"

"Sure, I know better than that," Will agreed.

"This lack of understanding of the human condition creates much turmoil and hypocrisy in society. We blame others for their mistakes but fight back when others point to ours. We attack ethnic and religious groups that are unlike us yet praise our groups for the same hard work and family values that we deny others. We boo villains and praise heroes. Then get angry and confused when our heroes show their moral failings. We fail to acknowledge the humanity in our enemies. I could go on and on."

"Wow. I can see that. We make things more difficult by attacking disagreeable people for the internal struggles that all of us face," Will said.

"Now, I will blow everything up, and we will reassemble this theory properly."

"The funny thing is that somebody may have made up or changed the story about the two wolves. It's fiction. A Christian speaker may have appropriated it for a talk he was preparing[v]. There is little evidence of this story in any Native Indian cultures anywhere. How does that make you feel?"

Will thought, "Well, disappointed because if it's fiction, then I can't...."

"And that is another issue with humans. You can't see the truth when lies surround it. There really is a war raging inside of each one of us, and we are lying to ourselves that is not happening. If confronted by the truth, we poke holes in it until it sinks. Then we don't have to accept the reality that we must change so that change can happen around us."

"What? You told me a story I thought was genuine. And then ruin it for me. Then you tell me to believe it as true. I don't understand," Will complained.

"The two wolves story is a universal idea told in countless stories throughout the ages. Every person has had to choose whether to become good or bad. For some, it's unthinkable to become evil. For others, that is all they know."

"In the Bible, Cain killed Abel for being good. The Egyptians tried to kill Moses to prevent the liberation of the slaves. The Romans crucified Jesus Christ for his beliefs. Superheroes, like The Hulk, Iron Man, Thor, & Spiderman, made personal sacrifices to battle supervillains. In Star Wars, Luke Skywalker decided to choose The Force over the Dark Side. Frodo the Hobbit casts the ring of evil into the fires of Mordor to save Middle-Earth."

"Okay, so the battle between good and evil is a universal truth. Why that particular story?" Will asked.

"This story helps me teach about internal conflicts, so I use it. On the other hand, it helps me show you how to question everything. Do not accept ideas blindly from preferred sources and discount information from your enemies. Allies can tell lies, and foes tell the truth. Don't always agree with my words just because you like me."

"Abandon concepts like wealth, power, beauty, and even intelligence as indicators of truth. Just because someone has authority, belongs to a religious organization, wears a suit, or has lots of praise from the community does not mean they cannot be capable of evil and malevolence. A modest and simple person of no significance can be of great character & moral support to you. Appearances are deceiving."

"Learn to think for yourself. There may be immeasurable grains of truth inside of lies. Some truths may be relevant to others but will fall apart for you under closer examination. Many ideas used to work but are no longer in fashion. Are they lies or just mistakes? Judge people based on their code of conduct, their actions, and not solely on appearances and reputation."

RULE OF PRINCIPLE 1: *The fates do not determine your destiny. You do. Choose to feed your soul's kind side, shun evil, and your Lifebook will start to fill with stories of joy, peace, love, hope, humility, kindness, generosity, truth, and faith. But fostering compassion comes from acquiring wisdom, and great knowledge comes from sitting with the masters of authenticity. To seize your destiny from the fates, you must mature into a strong & patient student of life.*

3. Tribalism-Nationalism - Shield Freedoms By Defending Your Enemies' Liberties

"When people look at you, they see a nice, mild-mannered man, knows how to fit in and get along with others. Your personality, training, and background make you an ideal family man and employee," assessed Morgan.

"I fit into many situations, but I am far more complicated than that," said Will.

"Exactly. Inside you is your dark side. This aggressive beast wants to attack without provocation and push forward to claim what is yours. You have descended from apes and other animalistic species, have you not? Yet you are also a tribal animal. A pack hunting animal that seeks others for protection and companionship."

"Huh, we are both aggressive and agreeable? Is that possible?" asked Will.

"Humans need to gather in groups and separate other people into yes, they are part of our tribe, or no, they are not part of the tribe. Many leaders find an easy source of power in exhorting their followers into a 'us against them' mentality. By nurturing hostility and distrust, each group separates and disassociates with the other.[vi]"

"But how does humankind keep group members from being aggressive with each other, you may ask?

"How?" Will responded.

"Each human has its dark side that fears and respects the dark side of others. We all want to have a purpose, accumulate wealth for survival, and be admired or respected by our group members."

"This creates conflict within. Do we fight for more wealth, or do we allow stronger members to take more and hold back our aggression?"

"When we challenge any leadership in a violent or verbal confrontation, we receive feedback that either we are in charge of the crowd, or leaders punish us for not fulfilling our roles as a follower. These unpleasant stories & feelings prevent us from repeating costly mistakes, and our self-regulation allows leaders to avoid using physical pain to force us to do what they want[vii]."

"So we are kind of captives to our dark side. We have no free will?" asked Will

"Not exactly. Your dark side manipulates you into doing things that obstruct your happiness. It also gives you the power to stay alive. Where do you think you find the inner strength to hunt a deer, fight off predators, or run from storms? The duality of your light & dark sides,*" explained Morgan.

"It is both our light and the dark elements that attract us to join groups for affiliation and survival. We get married because we both love someone and fear the isolation of loneliness. Soldiers join armies to have adventures and to rage against the world. Workers find work to build a family and to avoid homelessness."

"So if I dwell in the shadow side of my mind, I will think up all sorts of problems of anxiety, fear, arguments, worry, and depression. If I think powerful and positive thoughts, will it bring up happiness, calmness, friendships, confidence, and joy?" asked Will.

"You do have the talent to simplify ideas to their best elements! Yes, that is the key idea that you must learn. You are in charge of managing your emotions and making life choices that encourage the kind of inner and outer world that you want to live in," said Morgan.

"Very few people know about this philosophy of being?" asked Will.

"Not many. We can't see the shadow in ourselves, but we can easily see other people's dark side. Without spiritual guidance, the average person invents stories to guess what makes evil possible[viii]."

"Some think that criminality is caused purely because of genetic defects. Others completely blame parental influences. Many conjure up the possibility of demonic possession to explain murder, assaults, and addictions." said Morgan. "There are countless factors that contribute to the development and destruction of one's personality."

"What causes someone to go bad? To murder, rape, or assault another person?" asked Will.

"We will talk about that later," dismissed Morgan. "Let's talk more about tribalism. Like attracts like. Your dark side is attracted to the dark side of others. Your light side seeks the light in other souls."

"When we participate in sports teams, schools, and political parties, there may be many reasons to do so - hope, improvement, friendships, and fun. But we rarely understand the consequences of our actions. Every tribe's culture can have a profound impact on our thinking and to fit in and belong. We adopt this culture as our own."

"So even positive organizations like charities, cultural groups, and sports teams can trigger our dark side?" asked Will

"Have you ever engaged in gossip within groups of positive-minded people? Have you avoided or snubbed those you did not like? Maybe given volunteers unpleasant work you did not favor? The shadow does not take vacations or rests. It's with you, lurking in the background, every second of every day you are alive."

"Understand this. Group tribalism is mostly positive and favorable. It gives you a sense of pride and belonging. You have a better grasp of your sense of self and identity when you belong to a large group of like-minded souls."

"The problem is that many do not know who they are. People let their personalities become sublimated & adapted to their preferred groups. That's when the leaders start making decisions for them. The gifts of their individuality get lost in a sea of conformity and groupthink.[ix]"

"When different tribes clash with each other, and there is very little or poor communication, tribes or nations start to imagine the worst about the "those bad people" and make assumptions about their behaviors, values, and intentions."

"Innocent actions can appear threatening, and it puts the other side on the defensive. Misunderstandings are how arguments start, or fistfights break out among sports fans."

"I believe you. I have seen it myself. Tribalism can happen in university departments, within political parties, inside tech companies, in church groups, or anywhere people gather." stated Will.

"Finally, when you assume the worst about people unlike yourself, you start to tune out what they are saying, argue to exert your point of view, and even dehumanize them so you can justify further harsher punishments. **Extreme tribalism leads to poverty of the weaker group, exclusion from commerce and politics, and sometimes violence and genocide."** Morgan concluded.

"Well, thank you for these stories."

Morgan got up from his chair and handed Will back his sports section. "Thank you for allowing me to bend your ear. We can keep going. I will be in touch."

"I don't have your number," Will yelled at Morgan's back as the elderly man exited the dinner."

Strange man. Smart but strange. Why was he so interested in teaching Will this stuff?

RULE OF PRINCIPLE 2:

1. *Do not pass laws that exclude or harm groups based on gender, sexuality, race, age, religion. Do not allow legislation that elevates one tribe over another in the name of protection.*
2. *Arrest or convict those who physically injure, rape, or kill others or damage and steal property.*
3. *If people are doing things that make them happy, and do not interfere with your property rights, allow them the freedom to make their own life choices.*

{To minimize confusion, all future chapters featuring Morgan shall describe a series of wrongdoings or criminal acts. At the end of each chapter, the author condemns this by proposing a moral reaction called a "Rule of Principle." A principle is an internal ethical belief of right and wrong, while a rule is an external societal force with benefits for obedience and punishments or penalties for breaking it.}

4. Night 2 SETBACK

Most people would say Will had an ideal career with excellent prospects. He was not so sure of that after twelve years on the job. It was almost like this man was a house cat stuck on a tree branch, neither being able to climb up or down. Will was stagnating in his job, and he had few satisfactory answers to this feeling of malcontent.

Senior management canceled another project. The client had pulled out at the last minute, and the engineering team had gathered at the local drinking establishment to grouse over their bad luck.

Will realized that he was hanging onto his job, the way he tried to keep his failing relationships going. He thought of Liz and how he tried to stay together with his ex-wife, even when the future looked bleak & hopeless. He was repeating the same thing with his career - it was time to go, but he could not see anything better out there.

When a couple tries to close doors on each other for some breathing room, they realize having a flawed portion of a loved person was ultimately a sweeter existence than the bitterness of romancing the wrong person.

Finding a soulmate in a sea of potential partners that were all wrong for Liz and Will would be a monstrous task. Neither of them could bear jumping into those frigid waters without an arm to pull them back out again. So they cheated on each other until staying together became more painful than splitting apart.

It was completely irrational, but Will felt like the client had cheated his team by promising the world and snatching it back at the last second. A betrayal of their emotions and enthusiasm that felt like another breakup! All that work went down the drain. It was unlikely that the client would come back to relaunch the building construction in the future.

One of the engineers made an off-handed remark that implied Will made a critical mistake that influenced the reversal, and witnesses could see Will's eyes shoot daggers of hate at the back of his attacker's head. Still, he said nothing.

5 Hierarchies - Protect The Powerless Despite Your Vulnerability

Will had burned the last of his weed. His eyes were heavy, and he felt that he was going to crash. Eyelids fluttered as he struggled to get up off his couch to the bedroom.

What the hell? He saw Morgan sitting in a sofa chair across from him, the same suit as yesterday. "Hey, what are you doing here? How did you get in?" mumbled Will, drooling on his shirt.

"You invited me. Don't you remember? You said come on by whenever you can. That's what you said last night in the restaurant. So here I am!" replied Morgan.

"I don't remember anything. How? Huh. Did I let you in? Can't remember you knocking or anything…" Will struggled to figure out how this man ended up in his apartment. Was he so high that he completely forgot to invite his new friend inside?

"Aren't you going to offer me some of your ganja? I bet you have some pot in your kitchen drawer," asked Morgan.

"Am I going crazy?"

"Nah, you are all good; I was just messing with you."

"Do you still want some…?"

"That's all right. I don't partake. Do you want to talk some more about what we discussed last night?"

"I got nothing better to do. Go ahead."

"Not many are willing to get into the tough subjects I like. You have watched those nature channels, right? Packs of animals sort themselves into a hierarchy of sorts when the more aggressive males or females take control over their group by winning battles and defeating the lesser rivals."

Humans also have a status hierarchy in which we learn our placements by watching language and body posture, rather than fighting for position. Far below our thoughts and feelings, we all know our place within the group and in society, and our dark side makes us fight like hell to ascend or stay where we are on the ladder.[x]"

"Hey. I got that. Unfriendly managers were sabotaging my climb up the corporate ladder. It felt like a personal insult to my value as an employee," Will had a revelation.

"Exactly. Simple things like insults, mocking, bullying, snide remarks, smug looks can trigger these primordial feelings within our dark side because the hardened memories of our ancestors are deep in the crevasses of our brains."

"Just as pack animals exist in social structures, low-status human males and females within tribes and villages historically received the worst places to live and low-quality food while high-status men and women received the best beds, meat, food, and partners.[xi]"

"Your usefulness to your tribe or family could be a factor whether you lived a long and prosperous life or not. Verbal attacks by modern man can cause the same emotions as our ancestors felt when attacked with spears. We fear to be seen as weak because our tribe could force us out of the shelter and into the rain, so we angrily defend ourselves no matter what."

"Wow. If we get into misunderstandings and fights, we might feel like our lives are at stake?" stated Will.

"Yes, heredity partially programs our minds, so we live as our parents and grandparents did. If your parents have a history of dominancy on the status hierarchy, you will naturally emulate them. You might live confidently and see the world as a resource to benefit your family."

"On the other hand, if your parents were fighting to feed and clothe you before and after birth, you may repeat these same behaviors. Because this stress is pre-programmed into your mind, you might continue to struggle throughout your life as well.[xii] This does not mean failure is inevitable. It just means overcoming negative thinking might be more challenging for those on the bottom."

"Those highest on the status hierarchy like kings, generals, and celebrities will receive more negative feedback like insults, criticism, and hatred than anyone. They can ignore most of it because their secure position makes them hard to attack."

"A low-status person like the homeless or refugee will feel very insecure, so it's much easier to trigger anger, resentment, and hatred in them by any negative interaction from anyone above them in the status hierarchy."

"That is brilliant. Things make so much more sense now," said Will.

"Now let's talk about those who are at the bottom of the ladder because they have no rights, freedoms, or choices. Did you know slavery is still a huge problem for humanity?"

    i.   "In 2020, forty million slaves, sex workers, or bonded laborers are working in every country, receiving only room and board or just enough wages to pay off their debts.[xiii] Legally free; these workers might have oppressors or masters who force them to work in factories, as servants or prostitutes. Some are watched and monitored by armed gang members. Others are manipulated through debt obligation or abuse to honor their exacting work contracts."

"It's our greed, anger, hatred, and laziness that coerces those in power to force disempowered workers to do the hard, unpleasant, unsafe work they don't want to do."

"When the legal authorities try to move in, they are moved in the middle of the night to secret locations. Their ownership rights can be bought and sold on the black market; slaves are carried in mystery by trucks, small boats, and in cargo ships and are often beaten, raped, and verbally abused by their criminal gangmasters."

"Forty million slaves and bonded laborers? That's like one in two hundred humans. What do slavery and status hierarchies have to do with each other?" said Will.

"Good question. Turning people into property establishes a minimum safety net for the owner and everyone who is already free. The slave owner never has to worry that he is at the bottom of society. The slave is. The slave also ensures that the owner never has to perform unpleasant work like cooking near a hot stove, cleaning the bathrooms, tending to dirty animals, or picking crops under the hot sun. If no longer needed, the slave is a form of wealth that one can trade for gold."

"Why is human slavery no longer a dominant form of property in the free society?" asked Will.

"The wealthy, actually everyone, has billions and trillions of slaves that serve them. You may know it better as cash, currency, and money. Property owners send out all this cash searching for profit, and these slaves go to work for them.[xiv] Earning returns on investments, hiring people to run their companies, turning land and raw materials into roads, buildings, airports, trucks, and ships."

"Money is the force that allows humans to live without exerting physical labor or forcing others to perform the work for them. It goes out into the world, into the stock market or private businesses, and returns with even more metallic or paper slaves for its owners."

"That is the second reason most humans abandoned human bondage as a wealth-generating tool; money is more fluid, transparent, and exchangeable than people. It does not care who the master is or what you ask of it."

"Those who know how to accumulate capital and climb the status hierarchy ladder can purchase safety, stability, influence, power, friends, and almost anything the mind can conceive of."

"So civilization did not give up slavery completely out of moral concerns such as human rights, altruism, and compassion? What was the primary reason?"

"Technology. Machines are vastly more efficient at physical labor than man or beast. But who said civilization gave up all slavery? **Some forty million captives remain. Slavery is among the most heinous crimes because while a thief may steal from their victim once, a master (owner) thieves hope and freedom from the slave every day from auction or birth until disposal or death.**"

"And if we are talking about wealth as the method to climb a status hierarchy, it's better to accumulate it than spend it. It is your moral imperative to speak out against worker exploitation and accumulate wealth yourself so you can construct the society you desire. Provided you don't abandon your values and beliefs in the process."

"Cool. Be good to do good." Will blew some smoke into the air.

"Ha, ha, ha. that is some pretty strong stuff, Will."

RULE OF PRINCIPLE 3: *Your position on the status hierarchy makes you feel vulnerable to monetary threats. Believe in something greater than yourself - ethics, religion, country, work, family - because it gives you a framework of rules when you feel lost & confused. Believing in a higher purpose gives you the strength to climb the social ladder.*

6. Prisons - Don't Assume Problems Are Solved When Criminals Are Jailed

The two men continued to lie about on the sofa. The television was on in the background, but neither was paying attention to those stories.

"If everything in the modern world was conceived of and created in the human mind, what is the original thought that made prisons possible?"

"That is a tough one! Justice? Anger? Vengeance? Fear?" replied Will

"All perfect answers. I was looking for the word 'Control.'"

"Prisons are a luxury of a prosperous society that wants to control both aggressors and their victims. Pre-civilization, the victim, chief, or king executed those who broke the tribe's rules. If spared, citizens banished criminals to the woods where it was likely they would starve or be killed by animals or rival tribes."

"You mean we are nicer to criminals by locking them up rather than have the public take vengeance on them? That is a pretty crazy concept to think about," Will remarked.

"You can see the problem of conflicts between families starting with accusations of theft, rape, destruction, and murder leading to immoral executions, revenge killings, and discord among the community. An authority like an army or police force must establish law and order to keep the peace."

"There can be no ethical code of order without punishment, and few alternatives to violent retribution are better than the punishment of imprisonment."

"Of course, justice has always been unequal and heavy-handed. Ancient royalty of classical civilizations built dungeons and cells to lock up prisoners of war, foreigners, thieves & vandals, and other royal family members and rival countries. Not for justice but for power."

"The execution of too many prisoners was not in the ruling class's best interests due to monetary costs. On occasion, the Lords showed mercy to gain respect from their subjects, and other times they just wanted to demonstrate their power, so they did what they wanted with prisoners."

"Unfortunately, just as our dark side can corrupt laws, our prisons are contaminated as well. In many nations, the innocent occupy jail cells in more extensive numbers than you think."

"I know. If you are saying African-Americans, Latinos, and Native Americans fill our prisons far higher than their proportions to society, many people are too busy to care," Will said.

"Too many are living under the assumption that prisons around the world are full of violent criminals who deserve to be there, and we need even more prisons & harsher punishments. It's not that simple. That belief is not going to solve anything and trick taxpayers to dump more money down the drain[xv]."

"I hate challenging the prison system because it does keep criminals off the street. Some criminals are so violent and destructive to the community; they deserve twenty to forty-year sentences, even life with no parole. To protect the freedoms of the innocent, we must restrict the rights of the guilty."

"Having said that, the criminal justice & prison system in most countries are highly corrupt and mismanaged. And why do we care about this?"

"Um, anyone could land in prison if they cross the wrong people or make poor life choices. By protecting prisoner rights, we are protecting ourselves from false arrest and potential abuse?" Will guessed.

"Excellent answer. Suppose every sector of life, from work to church to politics, became morally bankrupt from influence peddling. In that case, affluent families could destroy their enemies by calling their loans in, stealing their assets, and having them imprisoned. We, the public, need to guard the criminal justice system against such treacherous power."

"Our current justice systems' negotiated plea deals, judgments, and sentencing can be very unfair and unjust.

We know the courts are a 'pay per play' place where deep pockets can buy you a great lawyer and shorter sentences. Wealthy lawbreakers can get small fines while broke criminals face lengthy jail terms for similar crimes.[xvi]"

"Minorities like African-Americans, Latinos, Asians, and Native Indians are arrested and sentenced in much larger numbers than their fellow white citizens, and this is not because they are more dishonest than whites. Poorer citizens are monitored and charged in higher numbers because police officers patrol certain cities more frequently than wealthier suburbs."

"The police have to go where the action is. Maybe officers are overworked and underpaid," Will explained.

"Fine, so the justice system is a bit racist & sexist. Courts should weed out the innocent from the guilty, but they are overburdened by demands as well. Judges may be extremely knowledgeable about the law, but let's admit the bias of their parents' moral indoctrination shows up when they issue judgments very quickly.

"For example, white men are given longer sentences for the same crime than white women. African men receive harsher penalties than all whites, and Republican judges give tougher sentences than Democrats[xvii]." Morgan took a breath. "I would also like to mention that if an accused person faces a judge who is tired or hungry, he or she will be locked up much longer than a well-rested or fed judge. This unfair application of the law is not very ethical to me."

"Again, this might be tolerable if all the evidence was sound. Many trials have unjust outcomes. Some accused were identified by mistake by witnesses and are serving time while the guilty run free.[xviii] Other criminals took plea deals without legal representation or by coercion from the officers and prosecutors."

"A few cases have been thrown out because of tampered evidence. But those are the exceptions, not the rule. Some gang members will confess & do time for the person who committed the crime. And of course, countless numbers of mentally and physically disabled citizens are arrested and imprisoned when the law should have protected them."

"It sounds dreadful. Very few leaders are criticizing the justice departments or the correctional system. Why is that?" Will asked.

"For fear of looking weak on crime. No politician in their right mind is going to speak out for the rights of prisoners. It will cost him or her votes."

"The United States has five percent of the worlds' population and twenty-five percent of the world's prison population. That's two million inmates plus seven million on parole. Every other country has similar crime rates but far lower incarceration rates, so why this crazy statistic?"

"People worldwide believe that if we expand the prison system, we can reduce criminal activity. The United States is a nation that can afford to test this theory. Unfortunately, while the threat of real jail time is very persuasive to deter honest citizens, it does not scare real criminals."

"Cons do not worry about getting caught until they get arrested. All claims that this overbuilding of prisons obstructs crime are nonsense. More jails mean more minorities are spending their lives going in and out of the prison system."

"Everything I said so far is a little outrageous. What I am about to tell you will blow your mind due to this sheer disdain of basic human rights."

"What is it?" Will was curious.

"Most Americans don't care who runs the prison systems. They are unaware that correctional facilities' privatization to secretive corporations has been a horrific lapse of judgment.

"These businesses are running prisons like sweatshops, employing cons on assembly lines at pennies per hour while collecting their regular fees from the government, your tax dollars. As they seek to increase profits, they slash costs by employing fewer guards, degrading meal quality, and stuffing inmates into cramped jail cells.[xix]"

"Many prisons are falling apart due to maintenance issues. Heating and air conditioning malfunction regularly, and many sinks and showers lack water. Mismanagement turns the facilities into a literal hell for prisoners. If you claim you don't care, remember some inmates are falsely imprisoned, and others have committed minor crimes like spraying graffiti or having unpaid bills they could not clear. These inmates don't warrant such harshness."

"Prison corporations want to maximize profits, so they request further government funds and additional prisoners to be placed under their care. Imagine executives getting excited more cons forced to endure tougher sentences so they can fill their pockets, and your mind has glimpsed inside the devil's playbook itself."

"As I stated last night, it helps to possess a progressive, open-minded view of the world because you will let new ideas in that others can't accept. Some other students would hear my rants of injustice within prisons, business, education, and religion and become angry themselves."

"Immovable to the immoral activities within the societies they admire and belong to; they are relentless in their misguided attacks on immigrants, other religions and age groups, the wealthy or poor, men or women, gays, or straights as the source of their problems."

"You have got to acquire the ability to observe dishonesty, corruption, and theft can happen in all industries, by any person, anytime; otherwise, you will run blindly into a maelstrom of betrayal by the very people you unreservedly give your trust to."

"That's enough for today. We will continue tomorrow." Morgan said abruptly as if he suddenly lost interest in the conversation.

"But…" Will protested

Will found himself awake in his bed again. His bedsheets and blankets felt heavy on his body as if made out of a thick tarp, so he pushed them off quickly and sat up. Will instinctively reached for his wallet to check on his cash.

To his shock, a picture fell out of a wallet pocket. It was a photo of two people smiling into the camera: himself and his ex-girlfriend, Angel.

RULE OF PRINCIPLE 4: *Do not enjoy the misfortunes of others, even if they are evil. Let criminals serve some hard time and fulfill their obligation to society. Forgive others for their mistakes because they didn't have superior methods of achieving their goals. Compassion for others is your way to be kind to yourself. Another way to see it, having resentment towards those who have hurt you is like drinking poison yourself and expecting it to kill your enemies.*

7. Night 3 SHATTERED

Will felt violated. As he stared at the broken driver side window of his BMW coupe, shattered on top like the Coastal mountain jagged peaks, he realized that his illusion of safety broke as well that night.

Should he go back into the office building? Call the security guard over to examine the transgression? Call his parents? Such decisions for such an unusual situation. Will also recognized that he was no hero when it came to a crisis.

He looked around the parking lot as if there were some clue that could crack open the case. Then he looked closely inside his car. The vandal stole nothing. Not even his phone and computer charger or his knapsack full of designer gym clothes.

The light rain beating down on his hair and onto the shiny nighttime surfaces reminded him that he was freezing and wet. Why did he forget his umbrella again?

Will ran back into the office and informed the security guard about the break-in. The elderly guard looked up and hurriedly searched for an incident report. What was the guards' name? Will did not know. He felt a little guilty for not learning who was who among his co-workers.

Resentment welled in him, a tightness in his chest, for suffering the indignity of this inconvenience. Why was this happening to him? He was a good guy. Shouldn't jerks and idiots get their cars smashed rather than law-abiding citizens?

The security guard walked out to the parking lot to look, and Will called his insurance company. After sweeping the broken glass on his chair into a plastic bag, he got in and drove home. He was pissed off royally.

8. Rich vs. Poor - Envision & Build The Type Of Society You Want

Will sat in his warm rental car, sheltered from the cold wind blowing around him. He was debating whether to go back into his apartment after a long day at work. He had stretched his six o'clock finish to eight, and that gave him ninety minutes before his usual ten o'clock bedtime.

He became fixated on the park's swing and then stared long and hard at the apartment window. Out of the corner of his eye, he saw he was no longer alone. Morgan was in the passenger seat of the Buick.

"What the hell? Damn it, man, you almost gave me a heart attack," he yelled.

"Sorry about that. It seems like you were thinking about staying in the car, driving around until bedtime?" Morgan observed.

"I still don't know how you got in here. The door did not even open," Will wondered.

"Now that you have gotten familiar with me and we have some level of trust, I can confess my little secret. You dreamed me up. You created me to access your subconscious because you are finally ready to take the next step."

"Liar! What kind of game are you playing?" Will yelled.

"Will, you have not slept well in three days. Your mind struggles to perceive the difference between the thoughts in your head and the real objects around you. That's what hallucinations are. An imaginative creation of your mind placed in a physical & semi-awake state."

"Who is hallucinating? Me? Are you trying to pull some scam on me? Who are you? Will demanded.

"I am a visual image of what your subconscious would like to represent to you. Part of you wants to climb out of this pit of anxiety, so you made me out of nothing, and I am here to show you a thing or two."

"You are a hallu..hallu..imaginary friend? Why is this happening to me?" Will was overwhelmed with confusion.

"It looks like your subconscious wants to communicate with your conscious mind, and that's why you conceived me. Even though you are the creator, you are resisting because you are fighting to maintain the facade of your current existence."

"Can you blame me? I am sorry, but I don't want to spend my life having conversations with hallucinations. I don't want to talk to you anymore!" he said.

"Don't worry, man. Before you know it, I will disappear, and you can get back to your ordinary life. Listen, there are things you need to hear, and we have a limited window to go over everything."

"When?" Will asked.

"When the time is right. Listen, you are exhausted. Don't drive tonight. How can you be allowed to keep working without your manager sending you home? I don't know! Let's just sit here and chat."

Will felt bewildered. "Do I have a choice?"

"No. The reason why we are talking is to unlock some of the mysteries of life. I will reveal many diabolical traps that others place in your path and how to avoid many temptations that will lead you to the dark side. You can then protect yourself, anticipate problems, and become so disciplined that you can even lead and advocate for others."

"If I created you, you have to do what I say, right?" Will protested.

"It doesn't work that way. If I could not confront you on your deepest fears and most egregious mistakes, you would wish me away and avoid dealing with your anger, anxiety, loneliness, and depression until doomsday."

"God damn it! Okay, fine," Will exclaimed angrily.

"Let's talk about the mayhem the top one percent of the economic world created for everyone else. The growing economic inequality and the disappearing middle class are the consequences of many rich folks taking reckless risks that jeopardize capitalism itself[xx]."

"You may not know that two-thirds of millionaires worked hard and intelligently to soar out of the middle class. They sacrificed many things to earn those yachts, mega-mansions, and penthouses in the sky. But there are also far too many wealthy people who have let their greed get the best of them. Their selfish drive to be the best and have the highest positions in their society prompts them to exploit others' weaknesses."

"Most affluent people are not so malicious and destructive as those who are campaigning governments to slash taxes, deregulate markets, minimize environmental restrictions, and allow wild and uncontrollable money market manipulation[xxi]. The silent majority step aside and let it happen because it would be irrational and foolish to interfere with their entire social group's upward movement."

"So a few trouble makers are gaming the system, and the rest are following them?" asked Will.

"Yes, the wealthy work to support each other, not just out of kindness & generosity but out of self-interest and affinity. The rich protect each other from outsiders. Outsiders like you."

"This separation of the classes creates different realities of abundance thinking and scarcity thinking. Even though the rich worry just as much as the poor, they think longer-term and make more rational choices than the stressed working classes."

"Rich and poor both use worry to help us avoid danger, predict the future, or plan how to respond to potential threats.[xxii] Worry helps us survive, but not necessarily to thrive."

"Teachers direct us to believe that low-income workers can't get ahead because they lack access to skills and capital. Not exactly the full story. What people don't consider is that putting marginalized employees under emotional stress causes narrow thinking to hunt for quick cash income rather than a more extensive game that yields huge dividends."

Will was surprised. "Are you saying that the elite is building a world where people feel disheartened and hopeless to kill their entrepreneurial spirit?"

"Not intentionally. It's a side effect, not an aim. Dismantling the middle class will decrease the pool of potential innovators & competitors for the establishment."

"There is no doubt, the poor have more pressure to find a minimum of food, protection & shelter, so there is a higher probability that their thinking is less analytical and more distorted. A relaxed and content mind can see the potential for commerce and opportunities that a stressed mind cannot.[xxiii]"

"Our minds are clear when we have a sense of joy and contentment, and this allows us to concentrate. If our thoughts are uncluttered with dangerous images, we can solve problems, create innovations in science, education, and medicine, and map out a fruitful future."

"When a poor person has unpleasant emotions, his shadow side will make him impulsive, jump at pleasurable activities like drinking or gambling, and will seek relief from his worries," said Morgan. "Had he had a 'can-do' attitude and energetic spirit, he might find the will to solve his problems."

"When a self-made millionaire has those similar negative feelings, he will see a red flag warning that he is on the wrong path. He might seek guidance, read, ponder, and then turn the problem over and over in his mind until he has a solution, or until the bad mood passes."

"But don't be misled by the idea that our dark side sabotages only the poor! The wealthy are also guilty of sloth, greed, gluttony, envy, pride, anger, and lust. While the working classes might be self-destructing before achieving their goals, the rich are also setting up their children for failure."

"When these heirs have inherited so much wealth that their investments provide all the income they need, they lose their drive to create, grow, and build new enterprises themselves. Instead of investing in risky new industries, the rich may seek slow & safe government securities, and much of the progress we have made will grind down to a crawl."

"Many corporations are funneling their expanding profits to the executive suite, padding bank accounts, or trying to crush small business competitors instead of sharing the wealth with all the employees. Additional profits come at the cost of wage freezes, carbon emissions, waste dumping, and inefficient resource management."

"If disempowered employees don't earn as much as they did before, they pay fewer taxes, which means governments have to cut services like schools, hospitals, road work, and policing. Some rich shareholders have lobbied to influence governments to lower taxes & deregulate industries to let businesses squeeze more production out of their operations and employees."

"Businesses choose not to locate or invest in these impoverished areas. As the economy struggles, the students in more disadvantaged areas don't receive adequate schooling. They simply can't compete with those scholars from wealthier towns for the best careers."

"The economic classes are now so detached from each other they live in separate realities and no longer recognize each other as allies in cooperation but enemies in competition."

"So the corporations are controlled by the one percent who hire the children of the wealthy in lucrative and stable jobs and then automate and deskill much of the other work for the poorly educated employees (and pay them lower wages). This cycle of increasing poverty for most and wealth for a few will accelerate until the system destabilizes and collapses. "Morgan paused and warmed his hands over the car vents. He smiled as if pleased that Will was a captive audience that could not leave freely.

"I just don't buy the idea that all wealthy families are selfish and do not want to help the rest of society. They are just as scared of the changing economic instability as everyone else. If we're going to make changes, we need to enlist everyone in this fight to redesign our society's morals and values. Rich, poor, socialist, capitalist. We are all in this together."

"Can I ask why you are talking about business & government corruption while all these murderers, rapists, carjackers, muggers, and bank robbers are running loose? Are they not the evil you speak of?" Will asked.

"We are discussing immoral institutional behavior because the average person is unaware that daily contact with such tricky deceit dissipates one's joyous life force, leaving many spent, bitter, and disappointed in their old age."

"Why are people so afraid of being ripped off by retailers, shortchanged by cashiers, or having their home invaded by criminals? These risks are in the hundreds or thousands of dollars in losses, and such worries are not worth the wasted mental energy."

"Contrast street crime to employers underpaying workers by thousands of dollars every year, governments burdening taxpayers with public debt, and advertisers manipulating consumers into overspending. Good people are losing fortunes because they are looking in the wrong direction at minorities, protesters, and immigrants instead of their leaders, who have betrayed the common good."

Will sighed deeply. He knew he was learning something privileged that was entirely out of the mainstream, but the young man vehemently hated feeling like he was falling down the rabbit hole like the book 'Alice in Wonderland.' Was the cost of this knowledge his sanity?

RULE OF PRINCIPLE 5: *Most wealthy and powerful folks are decent, but the rich who have shifted to the dark side are recklessly gouging the global economy and the planet's resources. Excluded from the meritocracy's ivory towers, ordinary citizens must band together to shame executive classes into curtailing excesses & worker exploitation from weak & corrupt moral principles.*

A person wielding power from weakness, anxiety, fear, and insecurity can create a considerable amount of damage. It is unmistakably unethical to be so greedy others get hurt, but objectors have failed to promote kind idealism into mainstream society's consciousness.

9. Law-Breaking - Being A Good Person Is A Reward Into Itself

The civil engineer suddenly found the energy to turn off the engine of his car and get out. Morgan also exited the vehicle and followed him along the pathway through the snow. The older man began speaking again:

Will, are you a materialistic person? Does your desire to own things control you to the extent that it consumes your thoughts?"

 "No, of course not," replied Will. "I buy what I need, treat myself occasionally, and invest the rest into my retirement plan."

"I am going to let that one slide. Let's talk about the relationship of power to the need to control people and things. It does not matter what kind of political system we are in - capitalistic, socialist, monarchy, or barter - cash will get you next to the seat of power. Lobbying is problematic because corporate donors can buy their way in to influence government decisions. Decisions that corrupt the free market."

"You do realize that the dark side in us compels us to ignore the rules and ethics in the institutions that enforce justice and fair trade.[xxiv] We can't say rule-breakers commit crimes from a lack of education."

"The corrupt can even explain the rationale behind these rules and can imagine the benefits of doing the right thing by playing fair. But many violate them regardless. They know but don't care. Their motivations of gain or destruction override the heart's capacity for feeling and caring.[xxv]"

"What a minute," said Will, "You mean wanting to own things cause people to break the rules? I could have told you that!"

"You are trying my patience," said Morgan. "What you need to understand is that old cliche that criminals don't know the rules is a lie that is not true at all. Additional education does not make a difference. Most rule-breakers do know the rules and break them regardless. The ignorant don't get far in this game."

"Oh, okay," said Will.

"So why are we learning about the topics of dishonesty, lying, cheating, and moral values again?"

"Um, to have a competitive edge so I can be better than people at having a more honest life?" Will answered.

"No, no, no, no! A thousand times, no! Did you hear yourself? Competitive? Edge? Better? More? Don't you think these ideas are contrary to what I am teaching you?"

Will was confused, "I thought you wanted me to win. What are you talking about?"

"This is not an area to compete with other people. If you want to be competitive, struggle with your old self to do better, and if you want to have more abundance, be more compassionate, kind, wise, and brave than in your youth. Being a good person is something you do in private when no one is looking because you are the only person who can hold yourself accountable to your deepest secrets."

"Ethical actions are, of course, performed in public because most misdeeds happen between two or more parties. You should desire that everyone wins, not just yourself. In the end, morality is about maximizing happiness for the greatest number of people, and elevating your status runs contrary to that."

"Don't you hate those who are moralistic, superior, and judgmental because they are rubbing your face in all their charitable and praiseworthy actions? Not a good practice. If you are letting your values become another status symbol to show a moral advantage to others, you are feeding the beast of envy, pride, and jealousy within."

"Being good is a reward in itself, a life of peace and harmony with unnecessary trouble on the run from you. Congratulate yourself on acts of kindness, but keep it to yourself without bragging. Do what's right, be grateful for the opportunity, and move on without a second thought."

"Bragging about one status is a form of insecurity, right?" Will asked.

"Right. The desire to show off or possess things comes from a fear of vulnerability and poverty. For example, many shareholders of corporations have a subconscious fear of future impoverishment, pushing them to demand higher rates of return, which forces large institutions to compromise their principles."

"Do you want to know how greed damages governments, cripples cities and impoverishes families?" asked Morgan.

"I am afraid to hear the answer," answered Will.

"Multinational corporations have unrelenting appetites to add to their wealth and influence, so they push their allies in politics to rig the system for their benefit. Corruption means lower working standards, tax cuts & growing deficits, reduced environmental and safety regulation, and wasteful bureaucracies in and out of government."

"So the dark side in consumers causes greed to spread, and these investors force corporate leaders to pressure politicians to slash government spending?" Will asked.

"….which hurt the poor and vulnerable the hardest, causing them to become angry and frustrated with the system. As justification, the wealthy politicians and corporate leadership become angry themselves and impede change in this conflict!" continued Morgan.

"Then the rich win again," said Will.

"No, the rich lose too because a feeling of a lack and emptiness still consumes them. The desire for riches is bottomless.[xxvi] Just like the poor, the rich want what they can't have."

Will reached the front door of his building and turned around to ask Morgan what he meant by that. His companion was gone.

Embarrassed, he looked to his left and right to see if anyone had caught him talking to himself. Utterly alone. He stomped his feet on the welcome mat to rid the snow from the soles on his shoes. Will fled the icy waves of frigid air and escaped inside his building.

RULE OF PRINCIPLE 6: *Hold yourself to a higher standard of morality than others demand of you. Being a person of high character is a form of spiritual wealth that enriches the lives around you. Many laws are minimum criteria that society demands and allow all sorts of wicked actions that we know in our hearts are wrong. Far too many are blindly running around hurting others because they were improperly taught right from wrong.*

10. Night 4 BULLETS

He never did it before. He missed thousands of opportunities in the past and never pulled the trigger. Today was different.

Will found himself asking the store clerk a dozen questions. How does it work? How heavy was it? Was it safe? Why could he not get it today? Was there a place he could try it out? The bored clerk patiently answered all these mundane questions as if he was on autopilot.

What compels an honest man to buy a gun? For some, it is just a tool for protection, no emotional attachment here. For other citizens, a firearm is part of their identity. Asking men to give up their guns is like chopping off their….let's say arm. Can there be a more masculine piece of metallic gears and polished wood than a fully loaded pistol filled with deathly cylindrical bullets?

In a harsh and ugly world where enemies abound, and competitors want to take you down, a man needs guns to protect his family and himself. A man is not a man unless he can step into the line of fire and fire off his shotgun to stop that evil force that would obliterate him and his lineage. Or is this a foolish fantasy that endures within a modern reality that has made such violence obsolete?

Something inside him stirred to select a Glock 22 handgun for purchase. If someone tried to mess with his car or break into his apartment, Will would be ready this time. So here he was filling out a three-day waiting form to purchase a nearly five hundred dollar weapon.

11. Advertisers - Avoid Buying From & Selling To Unethical Marketers

It was inconceivable how Will operating on so little sleep and still managed to talk, walk, drive, and work? Will did not understand how he was handling this feat of endurance. The engineer was too tired and numb to care. Will could sense the joy and excitement around him as shoppers walked in and out of retail stores around him. He just could not feel it.

Will stopped and looked through the glass window at some sporting apparel for skiers. He remembered sliding down icy slopes in his teens and relaxing in front of cabin fires.

In the reflection of the store window, Will saw Morgan standing right behind him. Why did he always wear the same familiar suit, tie, and shoes?

Morgan began talking as if they were already in mid-conversation, and he was answering a new question.

"Did you know one of the greatest fears of young children is being abandoned and left at the mercy of others?"

"I didn't, but I can remember sensing that in preschool and kindergarten," said Will.

"This deepest fear of the dark side has been exploited by the marketing and advertising industry for years. They may not know the exact psychology of how it works, but marketers are using effective techniques that persuade consumers to buy."

"So consumers are being manipulated to buy everything because of what happened in our childhood?" asked Will.

"Yes, Our society requires parents to leave the infant child for periods to sleep, work, shop, and tend to other activities. Children cannot understand adults' motivations and behaviors until they are taught concepts like 'work and responsibility.' Parents are sensitive to this distress and try to reassure their kids they are safe and protected even when they are absent."

"Interesting. Go on, "Will remarked.

"Some children cope with this necessary abandonment well and believe themselves to be valuable, safe, and secure within the home, school, or playground. They feel confident enough to make friends, learn skills, and start school because they can count on their parents' love and protection.[xxvii] Other children do not experience this and feed their dark side with thoughts of fear, anxiety, and worry."

"Often, the child mistranslates this belief into one that he or she is not worthy of the parent's attention; something is wrong with them. The child may feel neglected by their workaholic parents and become suggestable to materialistic coping mechanisms."

"Is this theory going to get a little wild? Are you going to tell me how materialism is a substitute for love?" asked Will.

"Great instincts. Yes. Parents also feel anxiety and guilt for having to work or choose to live their own lives. Parents and children can establish an unconscious pattern of sub-communication that makes parents feel completely guilty for the abandonment. Neither side says anything out loud, but they are showing discomfort in this uneasy relationship.[xxviii]"

"Remember, the personal values and norms of the family and community create this interpretation. In reality, the parent is doing the best she or he can but has unworkable expectations of how she or he should be behaving."

"And where does marketing & advertising come in?" asked Will.

"Marketers taught families, through advertising, that purchasing and exchanging material objects like toys, clothes, jewelry, and food was an indicator of love and affection."

"Parents who felt guilt could relieve this negative feeling by purchasing items at retail stores and then give gadgets to their children. Children learned to desire playthings if they see it everywhere. Their friends have it, television promotes it, and parents promise to get it for them."

"I get it. The child begs screams and misbehaves until they get the toy or candy. The parent manipulates the child by exchanging desirable behavior for objects of value, and the child trades quiet time for external rewards like toys." said Will.

"Yes. Advertising promotes a lie; those good parents should give the child as much as is required for a healthy and happy childhood. If Billy's Mommy gives him chocolate, she is a good mother, and Tommy's mother does not, Tommy received few pleasures of a wonderful childhood. She becomes a bad mother by default. If most parents believe this marketing to be true, social pressure coerces the remainder to fall into line."

"It gets worse. Children and adults are in constant comparison mode. They are very competitive, jockeying to see who has more stuff and who is more popular. Indulgent parents, who give their children the most toys and experiences, make them objects of envy and desire by other children. Our kids learn materialism elevates their status and reason for being."

"Advertisers have turned us into mindless consumers because we don't know how to be good parents, huh?" Will stated.

"It's not completely the fault of marketers. They move products off the shelves, and they figured out how to get consumers to buy far more goods than is required for their well-being. Now marketers and their families are also caught up in this materialistic mindset of substituting love, spirituality, and personal growth for mindless pleasure.[xxix] Everyone falls into this trap, even the instigators."

"The current generation of children receives a relentless barrage of ads interrupting their television, radio, and newspaper entertainment. Far more than their grandparents' generation."

"The worst aspect of advertising is that it creeps into every aspect of life- signs at the ballpark, ads in bathrooms, and social media posts. You see placements in movies, posters in every train & bus station, and constant interruption of work and play with emails, tv ads, radio ads, and video ads. Every ad steals some of our cognitive energy and wears us down."

"Advertising tells us our lives are not good enough, we have problems, and they have the solution. This manufacturing of discontent creates an increasingly unhappy population as they continue to acquire stuff or experiences that solve some concerns but neglect to convert their desire for transformation."

"Do you think it is going to be easy to be happy when reminders abound of all that you lack? People expect lasting contentment and better relationships by following the crowd but merely receive temporary pleasure and fragile friendships inside a rat race."

RULE OF PRINCIPLE 7: *Advertisers are exhausting our patience by magnifying problems and offering false solutions. The solution? Start or* *support businesses that treat customers better than that. Steal the customers of evil corporations by doing good in the world.*

Try not to sell unnecessary products & services to inappropriate, underage, mentally unstable, misinformed consumers. Place your community ahead of your profits, and you will receive spiritual and emotional rewards far more extraordinary than monetary gains.

12. Beauty Industry - Protect Children From Dishonest Vendors

Will and Morgan moved past the sporting store entrance and stopped in front of a brightly lit makeup store. They looked at a poster of an exotic and curvaceous model from the Mediterranean posing with some dark lipstick tube.

"When I see the shadows of humanity covering the earth, I know there is no chance for young women from escaping the clutches of the Beauty Marketing industry."

"You take all this anger, rage, jealousy, envy, hate in each one of us, and we sublimate all this ugliness down. The natural reaction is to see physical ugliness as indicative of all the negative qualities we hate in others and pure loveliness as a sign of heavenly divinity."

"It's completely inexcusable that society denies average people opportunities to display their gifts and have fewer chances to attain the wealth, popularity, and admiration that beautiful folks get to achieve more easily," said Will.

"Life is unfair, and that is why strong leadership is required to help right some wrongs."

"Everything we have talked about are all factors **contributing to an industry that sells unattainable beauty to an audience who cannot satisfy their deepest fears that they are not enough.**[xxx]"

"But for now, I will share three reasons for the insatiable desire to become beautiful, and how it causes envy, the feeling of discontentment and resentment."

"Surprisingly, both narcissistic and authoritarian parents may demand perfection from their children. Anything that could embarrass the parents is a poor reflection on them rather than their offspring, so they punish their kids to the point that kids will only experiment in winning activities.[xxxi]"

"The children's physical appearance is essential as it reflects the reputation of the family name. The children are encouraged to perfect their makeup, hair, and clothing and receive reprimands if they fail to satisfy expectations."

"Permissive parents do the opposite. They allow the child to win arguments, steal freedom, and establish ground rules and expectations for themselves. Kids do not know how to pick and choose among hobbies, homework, and friends and easily fall for the beauty industry's marketing tricks. The girls of permissive parents receive compliments for their lovely appearance, and this gives them the esteem they desire."

"No matter how involved parents are, if they do not teach intrinsic skills like making moral judgments, then children will learn to overvalue the influences of similar children of the same age. Children should not be the dominant source of learning because they lack perspective and wisdom from experience, yet they often are.

"Many young women find strong acceptance from their peers based on their physical beauty. The queen bees undervalue the thoughts and opinions of their supplicants. Girls may hesitate to express themselves or do not confront bad behavior like shunning, bullying, and gossip against others.[xxxii]

"The girl pack's followers assimilate into the group and will capitulate to demands that they purchase comparable clothes, use the identical makeup, and style the hair as the rest of the group."

"I had no idea that teenage girls had it so rough," said Will

"Not just girls. Everyone. Older women, boys, and men have other priorities and desires, but they also fall under manipulative forces that make them anxious and unhappy."

"Magazines, media firms, fashion designers, and cosmetics manufacturers all unknowingly conspire to present an unrealistic image of beauty to men, women, and children. In a rush to beat the competition, win consumers, and boost financial profits, all these companies project images of physical perfection that no real human can obtain."

"That's terrible. Beauty marketers are giving false hopes just to make money," said Will.

"Young women in their teens and twenties are selected for their thin bodies, flawless skin, and symmetrical faces and then transformed by a team of experts into models of desire.

A few thousand beautiful women (and men) out of billions of average humans are dressed up, made up by makeup artists, and photographed endlessly. Any flaws remaining are removed digitally by photoshop software."

"The photographs and video footage look nothing like the real models when they walked into the studio. Who are the customers? Glamor magazines, fashion labels, clothing, and makeup manufacturers, and any corporation or government that wants to promote images of health and beauty to sell their messages."

"Most consumers already know about photoshop & digital alterations. I heard girls in the mall talking over a magazine how fake the images are," countered Will.

"Not all. Children of a very young age and the uneducated encounter images of perfection and start to desire to transform themselves well before understanding the concept of computer-enhanced imagery. By the time they realize marketing's reality, they have already established deep emotional beliefs about beauty," replied Morgan.

"Good point. So it's too late to educate our children if they observe cosmetic and fashion ads at an early age?" asked Will.

"It's never too late. This assembly line production of millions of false images negatively affects self-esteem and confidence in consumers. Buyers assume they are not attractive enough to make friends, win jobs, and find their desired romantic partner."

"Parents can counter this idea by teaching beauty, and thinness is just one of many qualities a young woman can cultivate to find her place in the world."

Two young women emerged from the store and gawked at Will, confused. Why was he talking to himself? He must be on one of those wireless Bluetooth phones. Any other reason would be too disturbing for them to contemplate. He stared back, and they moved away.

"Morgan. Where are you?"

Damn it. The apparition had vanished again without even a warning or a goodbye.

RULE OF PRINCIPLE 8: *Beauty Marketing is a deception gone too far because young girls & women starve themselves, undergo surgery, or spend small fortunes, trying to achieve physical perfection based on dishonest imagery.*

Liars hurt others but can't see any consequences of their lies. Try not to lie or deceive. You may tell lies to spare others' feelings but do not do it to steal or take advantage of others. Marketers may use deception & storytelling to make their products alluring, but using manipulation to trick consumers into buying is going too far.

13. Night 5 - BOREDOM

He had found a new level of boredom that he did not think was possible. Will was holding a

bottle of Jack in one hand and the remote in the other. Please make this night end, he thought. Usually, he would go to bed early, even at 8:52 pm, but he could not fall asleep. Not even alcohol was helping. All it did was give him a massive headache.

Will flipped to yet another channel in pursuit of some slight relief of his bland evening. Like a compulsive gambler playing the slots hoping for the jackpot, Will kept checking his smartphone for DMs and texts. Bingo! A sweet win landed in his box. It was a message from his ex, Angel, asking how he was doing?

When he met her three years ago, Will thought she was a genuine spirit from heaven. She was so sweet and beautiful to him. At least in the beginning. Fifteen months into the relationship, he thought Angel began acting demonic. Heaven turned into Hell, and he did not know why. After numerous breakups, they finally called it quits close to their second anniversary.

Will fired off a quick succession of messages. He had to know if she was in a serious relationship but knew better to ask directly. What kind of people was she hanging out with? Was she still an executive's assistant in a financial firm? Was she happy?

When Will admitted he was at the same firm after six long years, he remembered this was a sore point between them. Before they broke up, she demanded that he keep growing and changing, while he fought back with 'why fix stuff not broken?'

She replied that something was missing, but she did not know what. Angel yearned for more.

As text messages flew back and forth between Angel and Will, they discovered they were both in between relationships. He got turned on by a flirty remark, and the texts got a little dirty as they recollected all the nights they spent together.

A flood of memories came back to him, like a dam bursting with sweetness and warmth. He remembered the first time he saw her, the silhouette of her body, her long blonde hair sweeping down an elegant bareback, her tight behind in a canary cocktail dress. The minute he saw her, he had to walk over before she turned around to reveal her face. No other pair of sparkling eyes had ever held him spellbound.

After they wound down their goodnight texts, Will brushed his teeth, changed into his bedtime T-shirt, and flopped back onto his mattress. As he lay down, anticipating sleep, he realized that while his body was begging for rest, his mind was still racing. It was unlikely he was going to be rewarded tonight with deep slumber.

14. Bullying - Break The Cycle Of Aggression By Standing Up For Others

Will and Morgan were driving along on the bumper to bumper highway traffic. He was comfortable seeing Morgan showing up in the oddest places.

Will was surprised how quickly he was adjusting to this new reality of living. Years ago, the engineer would have fought harder to avoid seeing hallucinations and would have sought professional help right away. Maybe Will knew it was useless to resist something his subconscious desperately wanted to tell him.

As the traffic inched along, the two men passed by a high school building surrounded by teenagers and their parents. The after school basketball game had just ended at seven pm, and the fans were going home.

Will watched a bunch of African-American girls surround two smaller girls and grab their purses and bags. These six girls, maybe between sixteen and nineteen, threw the contents of one of the bags on the grass and ran away laughing. The two girlfriends stopped and kneeled to pick up their school books and supplies. Will looked aside in disappointment.

"Would you look at that? Six against two. Damn cowards!" remarked Morgan.

Will did not say anything. While he agreed with Morgan that it was uncouth behavior, he felt unsettled about judging younger people. Trying to understand them was like being a fish out of water.

Morgan did not take the hint. He started a new rant.

"Remember when you used to go to school? We used to shrug off bullying as a normal part of childhood. These days, many concerned parents and teachers have launched anti-bullying campaigns to reduce the number of incidents."

"What do you think happens to those children who pushed around kids in the playground? What kind of adults do they become?"

"Some become criminals, and others become bosses. My bosses," said Will.

"You are not far off. Tyrants grow up and attain authority to coerce, intimidate, and threaten their subordinates.[xxxiii] People who bully seek positions of authority because it helps reinforce their sense of self and allows them to act in ways that are in line with their organization's objectives. **Workplace aggression is an enormous sorrow for victims forced to work under despotic supervisors.."**

"Adults know what is permissible and what is not, subtle, silent signals of intimidation and dominance has replaced physical violence or overt verbal threats. The workplace culture encourages it because work gets done, and the managers can pretend this practice does not exist."

"Yep. I hinted at wanting some time off. My boss replied that my work was slipping in quality to the point that my annual bonus was in danger. When I canceled my vacation plans, he no longer complained about poor quality work," said Will.

"Many managers issue additional work and undesirable tasks to their newest staff or those who are least popular among the subordinates. While senior staff might assume this is a normal part of gaining experience in the workforce, the repeated hinting and threatening of demotions or firings turn normal supervision of work into a coercive activity."

"Tormentors will also pick on or criticize some victims for minor mistakes while giving their friends a free pass. As a result, many employees dislike their jobs because they don't feel secure and supported in their workplace."

"My boss assigned work to me that I think he really should be finishing. What annoys me is seeing him having wasteful meetings with his friends," said Will.

"The shadow of people you work with will always express itself in unkind ways. During times of stress and commotion, this tyranny becomes more pronounced. Your boss is trying to suppress his childish personality because he knows it's unacceptable. Still, this bullying will pop up whenever you challenge his authority or try to gain something from him that might hurt his reputation.[xxxiv]"

"I was not sure if he pressured me. It seemed like standard business management," Will was confused.

"Your intuition alerts you when mistreatment is going on. It may not be a boss. It could happen to anyone from multiple sources in the workplace."

"Did it occur to you that other workers might try to undermine you to secure their positions? Was your job under threat at any point? Did you receive the silent treatment when you needed help? Were there nasty rumors floating around about you? All these are forms of childish passive-aggressive bullying by other employees."

"How does the dark shadow manifest in the workplace?" asked Will

"Manifest? Look at you. Even if you enjoy your job, you must wear social masks every day to hide your fear & displeasure. You would rather that others not find out about your dark thoughts, desires, and impulses, so you hide your dislikes and upsets under a false smile.

"This repression of your true identity causes a stress buildup, which causes you to drink beer or smoke pot to release some tension out like letting air out of a balloon."

"That sounds like every soul in my office. We all do that!" Will defended himself.

"Of course, that is the work culture. As part of your evolution, you need to experience the ups and downs of life. You live as part of a divine plan that requires you to take on new challenges and fail more often than you like. You will be embarrassed, angered, and ridiculed by fools who don't understand you and those who feel insecure by your rise in status and power."

"'As you recover from these losses, wounds, hurts, and mistakes, your shadow will make you feel crazy, depressed, angry and confused. When you hide your true self behind your social mask, you defuse the dangerous potential conflicts you could have with others.[xxxv] Protecting yourself in the workplace takes up valuable energy, and that is why it seems many projects plod along at a snail's pace."

"Nevertheless, you will make slow progress towards your goals. Then the clouds will lift, and the sun will shine through. In the aftermath, this struggle reveals your new talents, joys, and blessings, and you can ascend, leaving those who were afraid to try behind in your wake."

"Wow. That is some way to describe the silver lining behind dealing with terrible people," Will said.

"The dark side of your rivals is both malicious and wise. It can see the potential in you and will do what it can to prevent you from overtaking them in the status hierarchy. Your dark side sees that move and responds with "tit for tat' (insult for insult, gossip for gossip, sabotage for sabotage) maneuvers in kind.

"But don't become paranoid & distrusting about your co-workers. Most are good people. They want to do their work and get home to their families. If you treat them as persons of high character, they will respond in kind."

"To build up your immune system, the spiritual kind, you would benefit from associating with good people regularly. Enjoy life and celebrate with the colleagues who treat you well. Get together to learn about their personal lives, their families, their hopes, and dreams. Avoid gossiping, backbiting, and the blame game. Try to meet co-workers at religious gatherings and community events so they can see there is more to life than paychecks and promotions."

"I like these ideas. If my colleagues knew me better and saw me as a real person, we might just treat each other a little nicer," Will replied.

"Now, you are getting it. Unfortunately, the work culture demands so much of us that it does not give us much free time for this to happen. Still, where there is a will, there is a way."

"Ha, ha. Very funny. Not." Will smirked.

RULE OF PRINCIPLE 9: *It is difficult to challenge verbal aggression behind closed doors by authority figures. Avoid keeping problems secret as that solves nothing. If possible, change environments and report the issue to their superiors on departure. If you can't leave, help children and other vulnerable people deal with their bullies.*

Counteract adverse work/school environments with positive groups that gather weekly or monthly to celebrate life, goodness, and community. Create happy events that welcome friends and foes alike, rather than engaging in the blame, gossip, and judgment game.

15. Workaholism - Please Don't Fall For False Promises & Exploitation

The traffic continued to inch forward. A bird flying overhead made a white deposit on the windshield, so Will turned on the wipers until it disappeared.

'So what can we do about it?" he asked.

"Workers don't know how to think and experiment. We lack the skills on how to deal with the BS and manipulation around us. Employees, sadly, decide the solution is to work until they can't anymore."

"Instead of fighting back and negotiating with their enemies at work, they give up too quickly.[xxxvi] The rising stars who know how to work the system can find plenty of anxious followers to do their bidding."

"When greed is stubbornly praised and normalized, all people, rich and poor, become slaves of the culturescape that endorses the work ethic that supports it."

"Are you calling me a slave? Are my friends' slaves? That is a terrible way of looking at our economic situation," said Will.

"Whoa! I said 'all people'. Rich and poor. We gain so much in exchange for tethering ourselves to the system. The price of leaving to gain freedom is often poverty."

"As for you, are you not tied to your computer most of the day? Yes, you can go home, shop online and get some free time to play but do you not work more hours than you would like, work with people you detest, think about work problems in the bathroom and while watching TV?[xxxvii]" asked Morgan

Will capitulated, "I'd wish you were wrong, but you are right. I can't escape my work."

"Those who unhappily work well beyond what is healthy and necessary to meet their needs are forced to make choices that prevent a fulfilling life."

"Managers give rewards of higher wages, better titles, and more responsibilities to those who work hard. They freeze wages, punish or fire workers who don't comply with unspoken expectations. It's a trap once you are in it because it's very challenging to change jobs or attempt self-employment," said Morgan.

"But this has always been this way. Working hard is part of life." Will pushed back.

"Is it? Are there not societies that legislate six weeks of vacations and forty-hour workweeks? Can you see that some tribes hunt and fish what they need and then rest and play the rest of the day?"

"We are Americans. Work is our way of being," Will said.

"And how did you get that way? Listen, if you want to combat dishonesty and see danger before it hurts you, you need to question everything, including prevailing norms and values. Okay?

"Okay," Will agreed.

"Had the culture evolved instead of fallen prey to our dark side, we might act of deep affection and regard for the well-being of others rather than obey fixed rules and laws that benefit some and exploit others."

"Oh? Your expression of skepticism reveals how strongly these beliefs about work have ingrained themselves into your subconscious."

"This socially acceptable addiction to work benefits the productivity of the organizations, owners profit from it, but they are bankrupting employees of their personal lives.[xxxviii]"

"So management is tapping into this belief in the American work ethic to get us to put in unpaid overtime?" asked Will.

"Yes, keeping employees busy removes them as a threat or becoming rivals. **The dark side of humans sees others as a threat to the well being of themselves and constructs ways to distract, occupy, and subjugate potential enemies while accumulating and hoarding wealth.**"

"There are millions of people who feel unworthy about receiving wealth and love. When they repress their shadow sides to hide their shame, they work even harder to perform, please others and appear perfect.[xxxix]"

"We are walking into work feeling incomplete, and discover work does not resolve this emotional feeling?" asked Will

"It's not your fault. When you were children, a poorly designed system of rewards and punishments trained you to obey. Not many parents gave adequate explanations to their sons and daughters why they received these behavior modifications."

"The mass of children made up their own stories of why this happened and filled the owner's manuals in their heads with behaviors they thought would maximize rewards and minimize punishments.[xl]"

"Many families taught unquestioning obedience to authorities, and someone would reward that hard work. Such beliefs created a pool of labor businesses that could overwork."

"All these factors contribute to a workforce that accepts assignments without question and does not challenge the system that steals away their lives."

"My parents taught me there is nobility in working hard. Besides, I am trying to get a promotion so I can save for retirement and maybe get married again." protested Will

"Corporations love to exploit highly desirable characteristics for their malicious ends. There is nothing wrong with working hard, long hours if you enjoy the task, suffer low stress or anxiety, and do not suffer dysfunctional relationships from such a workload. Many employees are paying the price, and not enough leaders are talking about it."

"Back to reward and punishment. Businesses have found motivating their workers with the threat of firings and layoffs is not practical. Instead, they prefer to sell the idea that anyone can be promoted. Advancement is more fiction than fact. Most businesses' culture and social structures prevent the average employee from climbing the ladder to the top."

"This is upsetting to me. You mean unless I do outstanding work, I might not advance?" asked Will

"Even that is not enough. Your personality & social skills must also be more acceptable to executives than other workers. The more pay and promotions you get, the fewer opportunities to move up as other workers at your level are equally intelligent, skilled, and hardworking as you."

"There are simply not enough executive jobs for everyone who deserves them. Many workaholics get stuck at certain managerial or professional levels. They are frustrated that their efforts are not moving them forward and incorrectly blame themselves."

"Alcoholism, gambling, and other vices accompany workaholism because workers need to numb their anger, frustration, and fear to cope with this stagnation.[xli] "

"Broken marriages and neglected children become so difficult to deal with that the workaholic doubles down on his/her addictions and job. And the managers at the top don't care to stop this bad behavior because it means examining the corruption and indulgence in their own lives."

"So once we get into a workaholic culture, we are stuck?" asked Will.

"No, unlike real slaves, you always have the choice. The problem is that these choices are difficult and painful. The higher you rise in a position, the more you must resist the lure of promotions conditional on additional work if you can turn down assignments selectively. Learn how to disentangle yourself from sixty-plus hour workweeks."

"Find out what work is precious and concentrate on that. Delegate the urgent and unimportant to underlings. Slash and burn all unnecessary meetings. Consider starting a business with employees that will replace your seven days a week job. Think, Will, think!"

"So, how can I put this into action?" he asked.

'Pull over at this traffic stop. I need to get out."

"What! I will do no such thing," Will protested.

"Come-on. Be nice, Will. I'm going to miss it if you don't stop right now!" Morgan said mysteriously.

Reluctantly Will pulled over, and he saw Morgan get out of his car and into a nearby liquor store.

RULE OF PRINCIPLE 10 - *People know it's easier to steal someone's valuable time than their money. Be aware and considerate of consuming the time of other people.*

Employers want you to trade time in your youth for very little money so learn how to increase your value as an employee to demand maximum wages. It's far more unethical than you believe in wasting friends' time or devaluing their work by asking for free things.

16. Night 6 - LOST

Will entered his bedroom and plopped down on his bed, sitting on the edge. He looks around the room as if he had never been here before. His eye line ended on a framed picture of his nightstand and his ex-wife, Liz, standing next to her parents. He missed those dinners with the Coopers, who happened to be the nicest people he ever met.

He compulsively checked his phone for new texts from Angel. Nothing since last night. The silence in the room was deafening, and he could swear he could hear the smallest sounds - the air moving around him, the ticking of the clock. Why was the profound silence so uncomfortable? Why did he feel embarrassed to live in this way as if deathly quiet signaled he lived a mortal existence?

He reflected on what Angel told him last night. This lovely girl had a series of handsome, educated, and wealthy boyfriends before and after their relationship. Several of them had proposed to her. Why did she not marry into such a life?

Because she told him, these intelligent men were fake-happy: grumpy and miserable at work, charming and lively while with her. She could forecast that their work-life would eventually bleed into their home life. She would sit in silence with her husband in every scenario, eating dinner together, yet utterly alone.

Will sent her a message and then decided to check in with his parents and friends. Maybe she was already bored with him and decided to move on? Soon he felt disgusted with himself for sending his needy messages, got off the bed, and went back to the squawk box to drown himself in other people's stories.

A message popped up on his phone. Yes, Angel wanted to meet in person whenever he was free. She seemed enthusiastic, and this made Will's heart leap. But who would show up on the date? The gentle maiden or the snarling malcontent?

17. News - Seek Beauty By Missing The News

As he entered the apartment, Will almost tripped over his barbells. It had been weeks since he had done any serious exercise. His life was going to hell fast. No girlfriend. No workouts. No nights out. And he no longer wanted to look in the mirror anymore. He was too afraid to examine his decline.

"Will, when you were born, did you decide to learn English, French, or German?" a voice came from the kitchen.

Morgan was standing at the door frame, holding up two mugs of steaming hot black coffee. One cup was for Will. His guest wanted the two of them to get comfortable for a serious chat.

"What kind of question is that? English is the language of my parents and the country we live in", replied Will in indignation. He took off his shoes and accepted one of the mugs before sitting down in his favorite chair.

Morgan sat down in the living room and continued his idea. "So the English language was the only option given to you. You had to learn it to survive, fit in, and accept what teachers taught you without question. You knew the beliefs, the schoolings, the collective dream of a society, and what the culture should be because parents and teachers gave one story to you to learn.[xlii]"

"I was only two or three years old. I did know what was going on," Will protested.

"Exactly. Would you believe that this society exists both as a reality and in a dream? The buildings, tools, land, people, laws, manners, dressings, art, and music are all a shared dream that becomes a reality. Leaders and artists submit different ideas to the masses, and the populace either accepts this as truth or rejects it as unacceptable."

 "Children believe in this culture very easily because they don't understand what lying, deception, and propaganda are. As children, we must believe the stories we are told with absolute faith because we are trying to discover our creative imagination is not the same as the facts and stories taught[xliii]."

"A dream that we share while we are awake and talking to each other? Will asked for clarification.

"Yes, your life unfolds as you think it exists. Your life appears as it is because we agree with each other what is happening. Almost everything you enjoy and benefit from was co-created in the human mind and can be unmade in the future. Even destroyed and forgotten."

If one person has a story of what happened and everyone else disagrees, that person could go insane from not knowing what is real and what is not."

"I think I have seen a movie like that. All the other characters judged the protagonist as mentally disturbed, but they all were conspiring to get his wealth."

"That word you used. Judgment. We learn by judging and comparing. We decide what is valuable and what is not so that we can pick and choose among limited resources, anything that will help us support ourselves, find friendships, build families, and create wealth."

"And what is one source of information that helps us judge the world around us? Will?"

"Have no idea. This story is a lot to take in."

"Newspaper journalism and other forms of news media help shape how we see the world around us. Journalists of principle understand their profession's gravitas because they know the stories they print help shape the reader's perception of the world. News organizations are partially responsible for designing the collective dream of what our culture should be."

"Journalism is not just about reporting honest facts about current events. Most newspapers, websites, and television reporting has been motivated by profits, sensualizing the most negative news to drive the highest ratings or most readers possible.[xliv]"

"On the positive side, journalists uncover just enough wrongdoings to keep politicians, educators, professionals, the police, and business leaders honest enough to keep the system from denigrating into corruption and ruin."

"The news is kind of terrible. It seems more like gossip about sports & famous people than legitimate journalism," complained Will.

"It is a reflection of the culturescape. We are like someone wandering around lost in a fog within a dream.[xlv] People are talking, and no one is listening, and if they do, they hear what they only want to hear. We don't know who we are, so when the news ignites waves of fear into the populace, we panic, worry, and forget to work on our highest priorities.

"We are living in a fog of fear? The news media created this fog?" asked Will.

"Yes, some of it. Do you understand this metaphor? Humans are so afraid of death that they wander into the fog where people gather to be safe. They become paralyzed by their greatest fears because they can't see outside the cloud of news. The most common fear is the fear of taking risks to be truly alive and to be themselves.[xlvi] This is why our dark side is like a shadow or fog. If you live like this, you are a pale imitation of what one could be."

"News journalism can either help illuminate our humanity inside this fog or causes us to freeze from the terror of magnified threats. Economic anxiety is shutting down much of the free press, and that may allow evil to spread."

"Once the free press is under authoritarian control, those without morals or a sense of right and wrong can run rampant by increasing this news machine to grow their power. When writers and TV newscasters abandon their sense of truth, justice, and morality in favor of ratings, everyone loses access to accurate and impartial journalism."

"Sensationalism forces the boring but important day-to-day community events and political doings off the air and back pages. Our dark shadow loves to devour its victims' misery, and audiences can get caught up in stories of murder, terrorism, crashes, theft, and political grudge matches.[xlvii]"

"This negative bias to report the worst aspects of humanity distorts the audience's view of the world. Bad news causes some observers to become worried, fearful, and anxious despite living in very safe environments. Their perception becomes a reality, and they forget how to live boldly and with purpose."

"You mean the news shapes my view of the world, and if the news is negative and pessimistic, my beliefs and actions become negative and pessimistic?" asked Will.

"In ways, you can't imagine. When populations become stressed and anxious, they seek confidence and strength from their strongest & most aggressive warriors and stop listening to those who preach wisdom and caution."

"The news promotes the loudest and most polarizing characters in politics because they get the ratings that news executives desire. As a result, the culture demands more immediate action on safety issues, law and order, and other matters that they perceive as imminent threats."

"This triggers a sense of injustice and anger for wrongdoing that was preventable had a higher authority intervened. Our intuition tells us those good people should be helping others when they are in distress, and that makes us feel shameful.[xlviii]"

"Had we learned how to marshal the resources of the community to solve problems, we could use the news as a source of information to locate those in need of assistance. Citizens could use various tactics to force politicians to act. We do not know how to use the news as a force for good."

"When we feel guilty about anything, it is something we know we did wrong and had the power to change it. Our culture makes us turn this guilt into shame because we believe our community is behaving immorally. We subconsciously feel shame as a people because we read or watch the news and fail to act to help those in need."

"In response, our shadow cannot accept such shame on our families and us, so we lash out at others. As much as we hate the news, we can't look away. We are programmed to scan the world for danger.[xlix] Instead of participating in the muck of the problems, we scapegoat immigrants, attack minorities, troll celebrities, and insult foreigners."

"No one wants to be the worst person in the room, so we go looking for more monstrous creatures that deserve more vitriol than us. The news media is happy to provide targets for us to shoot at, and we are happy to have one more thing to distract us from living an honest life[i]."

"We should avoid the news, huh?" asked Will.

"Just read the headlines. Don't let yourself get engrossed in the drama of the stories. Skip the news and go right to entertainment, weather, and sports. Start projects. Create an empowered culture of activists.

"If you have the resources to make a difference in your town or neighborhood, read community newspapers, and volunteer to fix manageable problems. You will gain strength, confidence, and respect by helping clean up abandoned yards or driving seniors around. Anything is better than doing nothing."

RULE OF PRINCIPLE 11: *News organizations can make their audiences ill with worry by portraying the world as much more dangerous than reality. Increasing anxiety in the population in the name of profits is sick!*

Please don't fall for media & news addiction. Avoid watching the news and do not associate with immoral people. These influences will make you see the world as a threatening and nasty place when there is so much beauty and kindness around you.

18. Fame - Celebrity Is A Dangerous Game, Tread Carefully

Will pondered this suggestion for a moment. He was a little distracted by the flashing lights of two snow plows moving some sleet off the road."

"Speaking of entertainment news, this is a good time to discuss celebrity culture. There may be no darker place on earth than the bright lights of Hollywood & New York," said Morgan.

"Are you serious?" Will responded.

"Just like a lantern hanging in the night sky is irresistible to lightning bugs, the entertainment industry attracts hundreds of thousands of actors, dancers, camera operators, writers, musicians and producers drawn to the flames of fame, fortune and glory. As humanity's sinister side is attracted to artists' dark shadows, they also seek to destroy the light of what they cannot be.[li]"

"What does this have to do with regular people like me?" Will asked.

"When you can see the shadow at play in one industry, like entertainment, you can see evil trying to steal and disempower in every marketplace on the planet. There is something about the pursuit of fame and fortune for actors and musicians, which is so powerful, that greedy vultures congregate among the world's media capitals to exploit and use these naive souls like nowhere else."

"Acting, music, art, writing, and dance are among the few places where artists can freely talk about the human condition without outrage and censorship. What cannot be said in conversation can be acted out in a play, and people can recognize our humanity in the performance and applaud with the audience.[lii]"

Will got it, "Okay, cool. And…"

"Some misguided or fearful parents believe the arts are childish and a waste of time. They want their children to succeed, grow wealthy, and climb the social ladder so badly these adults discourage their offspring from engaging in high risk-high reward activities that favor the beautiful for a minimal amount of time."

"Children under the age of six are allowed to indulge in fairy tales and pretend games because little kids can't tell fantasy from reality. As children learn the difference between imaginary pretending and lying, some fall in love with the arts and continue enjoying the wonders of playing characters or making music. Drama, writing, music, and dance are restricted to a few outlets for children's creativity and discouraged almost everywhere else."

"Some children grow up isolated, self-centered, or just odd. Their lives are full of lost opportunities to share, connect, solve problems, or develop social skills. Other children continue to live in fantasy worlds of their own making and fail to see the growing ruthless and exploitative threats around them.[liii] Their naive and trusting nature makes them easy pickings for the monsters who lurk in boardrooms and recording studios, waiting for fresh victims."

"Oh, now I see where you are going with this. Is it that bad?" Will asked.

"Perhaps not. The majority of the entertainment industry has high-grade moral character - most want to create. However, the money flowing into film, television, and music attracts many predators who want to con money out of the talent who are unfortunate enough to fall into their manipulation trap."

"Sounds ugly. Don't tell me that even my favorite singers and actors have fallen for this behavior," Will asked.

"In the beginning, yes. Most celebrities were not warned of these dangers and did not foresee the hardship of launching their careers. For young models, dancers, and actors, they have to run a gauntlet of tedious auditions, callbacks, photoshoots, waiting around, practice sessions without pay or guarantee of work."

"Some casting agents are cruel and exploitative and reject applicants for the smallest of reasons. Many producers and agents demand sexual favors from both male and female performers to get any audition role.[liv] Too many accept these terms and gain little in return."

"Tens of thousands of hopefuls travel to New York, Los Angeles, London, and other cities trying to launch their careers. Met with indifference and rejection, most drop out. There are just so many of them, and most are indistinguishable from the rest. Aging actors and models are pushed out quickly by new youth and talent."

'If you watched any film or read any book about the rise of rock and roll stars or actors, it's highly likely there will be some scene where the musician or artist confronts the manager for stealing from him or her. The film studio, record company, or concert promoter gave the manager more money than the musician thought they were being paid and pocketed the difference. It's now a cliche in Hollywood."

"Many celebrities who do survive this trial by fire find no gold at the end of the rainbow, and the money and fame earned were not worth the cost of their happiness. They reached the top by compromising their artistic creativity. 'Winners' lose themselves in the false image they created and no longer know what makes them truly happy."

"You make performing sound like a horrible profession. What about those celebrities that appear to be successful, wealthy, and adored?" Will asked.

"You are right. I have been focusing on the immorality of the entertainment industry when many entertainers have a wonderful time earning their 'happily ever after.' Plenty of performers do not find success here but leave the business unscathed and find their happiness in unexpected places."

"The raw and free displays of their talents may inspire the rest of us but also opens a pandora's box of shadow behaviors by jealous opponents. Outraged that we must suppress our desires to dance, sing, and express ourselves to fit into normal society, we attack those who can.[lv]"

"You witness the criticism, trolling, staking, mocking, censoring, and hatred of performers, famous and infamous alike? We repress those embarrassing and shameful ideas of what we want and scream in anger at those who dare to do what we can not. We study stories of the overweight celebrity, the failing drunk actor, the sex scandals, and musicians' drug addictions[lvi]."

"We project our insecurities and values onto actors and musicians, so many of us call them lazy and potheads. Crazy misfits who are so pathetic that they need caretakers to do the smallest tasks. Actresses are called sluts, male actors implied as gay, and we are astonished if entertainers show they are not stupid or indulgent."

"Let this judgment go. The worst thing you can do is kill someone else's dream just because you don't understand it. Allow young people to indulge in their fantasies and imagine becoming rich and famous. If they fail, they will have decades to work in regular, safe careers. This joy of creation and enthusiasm is a gift to the world, and we should nourish any expression of love."

"No parent should let their children work in entertainment without a mature and experienced mentor's guidance.

Young adults should prepare for the challenges of navigating a town of predatory agents and producers."

"Can I please go to sleep now?" pleaded Will. "I am exhausted."

"Why are you asking me? Okay, try to get some sleep. We can resume tomorrow.

"Will's friend disappeared into the bathroom and did not reappear. Will closed his eyes and realized that he was drifting into sleep. Ten minutes later, he opened his eyes and concluded he was in for a long night.

RULE OF PRINCIPLE 12: *Most criticism is self-criticism, so be supportive of strangers and friends, even if you dislike their work. Be your boss & create art that makes you cheer. Choose that which delivers you contentment. Pick the career you want, the spouse you prefer, and the house you love. Don't let others push you around based on the morality and beliefs suitable for them but do not satisfy you. Do not seek to destroy the dreams of others, for that is a monstrous trait indeed.*

19. Night 7 - REUNION

As Will and Angel traded additional texts, he realized that he was dying to see her in person again. Based on her athletic, blonde, and gorgeous, social media photos, time was not taking a toll on her appearance. Most men found her irresistible, and Will knew she could play around with him and toss him aside if she fancied.

It was extraordinary that he won Angel's heart three years ago while hanging out with another girl he liked. Why was his dating life either feast or famine? Women like that usually did not pay any attention to unremarkably handsome men with boring jobs.

Angel admitted that she felt envious of the playful banter between Will and his date. Using smooth words doesn't work on me, she told him. Men lie in bars all the time, but they can't hide their qualities while on dates, and other women see right through them. If Will's 'friend' could be enthralled with him, Angel decided on giving him a chance. Actions speak louder than words. That's why.

Angel texted that she was getting tired of sending messages. She preferred to talk to Will, face to face, and hear his voice again.

Will was overjoyed. Then he felt anxious and confused as he remembered all those vicious arguments they suffered through before the final break up. Did she want to have a hookup? Was he a rest stop between boyfriends? Or did she want to try again? Maybe she had matured and learned to control that hot temper? Could they make it work?

Despite his reservations, he called her. Boldly, she started the conversation by asking him to ask her out. Of course. This weekend, of course.

A world-class flirt, Angel, teased out the answers, slowly getting Will to admit he was very interested in her comings and goings. Did he still have feelings for her? she asked.

The feelings never go away. They just fade from a roaring rush into a dull whisper, he replied. She loved that soulfulness of his.

Will wished he had an enthusiastic confidant to share this gossip. His real friends, the ones he had serious conversations with, knew of his history with Angel and would have cautioned him to stay away from her. The engineer did not want anyone to steal his thunder. Angel was hot, and he wanted a piece of that action.

She suddenly interrupted the romantic chatter by announcing that she had a laundry list of things to do tomorrow morning. Could they continue tomorrow evening?

Will agreed. He had been up for fifteen hours himself and did not feel like dragging out the conversation. He had no more energy tonight.

20. Racism - Your Prejudices Will Corrupt Efforts To Become Good & Moral

Even though it was almost eleven o'clock and highly unadvisable, Will got out of bed, changed into a thick and layered tracksuit, and left the apartment. 'Who goes for a run in the middle of a winter night?' he asked himself. Idiots like himself, he replied. What an excellent way to start the year, he thought cynically.

As he slowly jogged down the street and into his local park, he saw a shadow walking towards him, partly obscured by the dark trees. Was he in danger? He recognized this person. It was Morgan, dressed in the same suit and coat as before.

"Hello, Will. Good to see you."

"I wish I could say the same to you," Will replied.

"Come on now, you know I am trying to help you stay out of trouble."

Will resigned himself to the reality that he was not in control of this relationship either. He would have to ride this out the way a fishing boat fights through a raging storm. The engineer silently nodded at his teacher to begin the lesson.

"You may not want to hear this particular subject because it cuts to the heart of our deepest fears of death and obliteration. The cost of becoming an adult is giving up one's childhood and going down this path requires the loss of innocence and fantasy.[lvii]"

"Prejudice and racism are echoes of our past when the fear of strangers and tribes made the difference between life and death. Our ancestors' memories embedded in our minds, we can feel these primal emotions when we encounter those who are very different from us.[lviii]"

"Are you implying my family has a history of racism? We are not like those other people at all." Will spat back in anger.

"Not at all, but you are human. Everyone is prone to feelings of fear and spite. No exceptions. The conscience of our minds refuse to recognize these unconscious dark thoughts because these ugly aspects are embarrassing and disgusting to us."

"We don't want to admit to feelings of superiority and racism because it's revolting and disturbing to those who know better, so we use other techniques to put other groups down. For example, we might deny resources or help to certain groups and claim they behave criminally or unethically because their activities don't align with the ruling culture's laws and norms. It's our bigotted attitudes that are the problem."

"The uneasy feeling of interacting with new cultures is a natural, emotional response to potential threats. It is reasonable to be suspicious of dissimilar people because it's fundamental to test strangers to decide whether they are harmless or not."

"There are always third parties outside this conflict who seize the opportunity to influence rational thought for their own benefit. Opportunist leaders make you feel that these outsiders are not safe so they can attempt to influence you."

"The belief that your race is superior to others is taught to the very young before children can judge whether that belief system is valid or not. Racists had no chance to escape their fate. Life forces that we can't comprehend, rolls a die of chance before they are born."

"Wow. That's an empathic opinion." Will remarked.

"We must acknowledge that all nations and languages hold prejudices against foreigners. Americans and Europeans focus on white prejudice against all other ethnic minorities since they control the modern economy's power and wealth. These stories are only part of the story."

Of course, minorities should be suspicious of cultural integration with those who control the finances and industry. They get burned over and over. Yet they need to make the first move & look in their oppressors' faces and see their reflections back at them. No one who is the victim of racist policies will admit that they might have similar beliefs to those attacking them."

"Based on history, every culture is capable of being tyrannical of their enemies. We see the English oppressing the Scots, India's elites mistreating the untouchables, northern Chinese slaughtering the Tibetian people, and Arabs infighting among their tribes."

"This means that if oppressed races were to take control of their governments, they might mistreat their former bosses and masters. We must recognize the dark side exists in all, and build institutions to protect ourselves from ourselves. While current power structures are hurting everyone, violent transfers of power could cause new problems no better than current issues."

It is very politically incorrect to say this, so very few journalists or writers will broach this subject."

"I knew this was true, but nobody has ever said this out loud," Will remarked.

"Well, it's a difficult subject to broach. In another lesson, I will explain why racism & negative prejudice helps spread evil but first...."

"Contrast an adult with prejudicial beliefs against a young child under the age of four. Children are free from the thoughts of adults. This child runs around with a smile, looking at nature, stories, and life with fresh eyes.[lix] If they encounter another child of a different race, they might run-up to each other and hug or play. When adults separate these children because of their differences, they might be surprised and confused."

"These children say and do what is on their minds. They freely love because they don't know all of the rules. The child learns the adults' laws, both good and bad, and gets programmed to obey. This knowledge comes at the cost of pure happiness and freedom.[lx]"

"The sins of parents become the sins of children. They take on the parents' fears, beliefs, abuse, and domestication as part of their identity. The circle is complete when they pass on previous generations' values and beliefs, good and bad, onto their children."

"While some intellectuals believe you can legislate against racism and teach equality in school, this is like waving a flag in front of a bulldozer. Character development must start from birth onwards. Children learn prejudiced behaviors from their parents and the community by modeling and watching others. This parental modeling is vastly more impactful than what is said by teachers and politicians."

"I believe it will take another two hundred years on a global scale to make systemic racist behavior a thing of the past, maybe longer. You can't teach it away. **Racial groups must integrate, help & appreciate one another if they genuinely want world peace.** In the meantime, some political and religious leaders will continue to use racist ideology to gain followers and advance their agenda to the detriment of us all."

"Why are we not talking about finding real solutions to our divisions on television or in newspapers anymore?" Will wondered.

"Your guess is as good as mine. Maybe it's politically incorrect to discuss something that is bound to be offensive to someone and causes the loss of reputation. It could be that opposing groups refuse to listen to one another, so why bother. My theory is that corporate advertisers have suppressed this story in the interest of marketing more junk. If the truth could cost them sales, they don't want the discussion to take place."

"Yes, when the lines of communication are closed, ethnic and status groups close themselves off to the richness of friendship and harmony. Our children will lead the way by befriending kids from other backgrounds: parents of all races will decide to coordinate activities together, and rapport will naturally flow."

"I hope you are right." Will paused for Morgan to continue and was surprised to see him raise his hand to shake goodbye.

"Better to leave on a high note than dragging it out. Bye, Will."

"Good night, Morgan."

RULE OF PRINCIPLE 13: *Prejudices turn good individuals wicked. It's challenging to a person of high character when our biases block out the virtue in other groups, and we see nothing but evil in their actions. Racism (and sexism) costs everyone because we deny ourselves great friendships, business partners, and talent from other cultures.*

Prejudice also nourishes and shields moral wrongdoing within races. If we are judging each other by our appearances and behaviors, we fail to see the immorality and evil doing by members of our shared race or sex."

21. Muslims & Christians - Religion or Traditions Do Not Excuse Child Abuse

Morgan and Will stopped walking and paused in front of a brightly lit up church. There was an enormous picture of an adult Jesus Christ staring out at all those entering this holy place right above the front entrance. He could feel like the eyes were staring right through him as if Christ could ascertain whether he had a virtuous soul or not.

"Many people avoid this comparison, but people of the Christian, Islamic, Buddhist, Hindu & Jewish faiths are quite similar in how they respond to the temptations of the dark side. The dogmatic response to other religions provokes the believer to act against humanity instead of embracing men of other faiths as co-conspirators against evil."

"I don't understand. These are five completely different religions," asked Will.

"Unless you are a student of world religion, you would not appreciate a large portion of the Koran & Torah, the Bibles of Islam and Judaism, shares similar scriptures and lessons as the Christian Bible. Despite these agreements, many Islamic leaders persuade their followers that Westerners and Christians are the enemy of Allah and apply this xenophobia to gain more power and influence."

"So like the Ten Commandments and the stories of Noah, Cain & Abel, Adam & Eve are inscribed in all three religions' scriptures?" asked Will.

"Essentially, yes. Now, remember, Christians have also waged war on Islam and other religions. Muslims see interference and meddling in Islamic foreign policy and commerce from America's government and other European & Asian powers. Manipulative and evil leaders tap into the dark hearts of humanity to magnify even small differences to turn tribalism violent."

"The majority of Americans realize that ninety-nine point nine percent of Muslims are neither terrorists nor support attacks against innocents in other faiths. Few Americans realize that Islamic subversives are killing far more innocent Muslim civilians than people outside their faith.[lxi] Behind the scenes, governments of all faiths are united in monitoring and protecting their citizens from terrorist attacks."

"So who is right and who is wrong?" asked Will

"When two drunkards start brawling, they are both at fault. One or both should have walked away before someone swung the first fist. So too, are all governments responsible. Christians, Jews, and Muslims alike."

"It's tragic that very few people do not see how the average citizen of their supposedly enemy lives every day. Christians do not see Muslims raising their families or building their careers, or engaging in volunteering. Many Muslims don't know Americans & Europeans personally, and they get a very distorted, incomplete projection of how their 'enemies' think and live through television and movies."

"If most of the diplomatic leadership perceives a political benefit to continuing the conflict between Islam and Christianity, then neither populace will see the true nature of their deemed enemy."

"That is very interesting, but what does that have to do with me?" asked Will.

"These religions have much more in common than you think. For example, both strict Christians and Muslims use corporal punishment to discipline their children and students. You were spanked and hit as a child, were you not?"

He caught Will off guard. "Um, yes, a little bit."

"More than a little. I know everything about you."

"Many children are slapped, punched, beaten, and whipped by parents to correct disobedience. But the children can see parents are getting drunk, arguing about chores, fighting over money, and misbehaving right in front of them. The parents are undisciplined themselves.[lxii]"

"Muslim and Christian children alike may receive words of love afterward, but they observe the hypocrisy of 'do what I say and not as I do.' Unconsciously, they know these words don't match the deeds of the adults around them."

"Strict punishment is effective so long as the parents are consistent, and children see that such restrictive parenting has real and long-lasting benefits for them. But vicious violence on the child causes them to go into their deep dark side and bring out feelings of shame, embarrassment, and humiliation. Then these feelings are repressed until they get triggered by outside forces."

"This happens to children in every religion?" asked Will.

"Humans are the same psychologically no matter where they live…. These children grow up with their sense of worth, responsibility, and caring being compromised. They may see the world as a hostile place. When the slaps and punches from parents come at random times, sons and daughters have no idea why they were hurt by those loved ones deemed to protect them.

Will asked, "And this trauma makes people emotional and irrational when viewing other nationalities and religions?"

"The child's response to being beaten, slapped, and whipped by parents is to run away, fight hard, or freeze in fright. Suppose other children or adults step in to stop or prevent this punishment. In that case, they may subconsciously decide to become dependent on others to solve many of their future problems."

"This behavior pattern will continue into adulthood, except they will overreact to threats of nationalism, terrorism, and immigration with fear and anxiety instead of rational calmness."

"Because home life was unpredictable and undisciplined, we grew up seeing the world as chaotic and strange. What is familiar feels safe and what is unknown appears to be dangerous. Adults who are sensitive to changes in their environment will react very strongly to meeting new cultures, languages, and personalities that they are not familiar with."

"When you say strongly, you mean?" Will asked for clarification.

"The dark side of both Muslims and Christians will open up with a torrent of abuse, intolerance, close-mindedness, and aggressive action to keep the threat away and shut down future interaction with this danger. It's that serious."

"Neither strict nor permissive parenting is the best strategy. You would rather not raise children to be disciplined hard workers but afraid to experiment, and you also don't desire free-spirited kids who never finish anything. Experts recommend a blend of guardianship where you are stern when it matters and more permissive when you want your kids to explore the world freely."

"Bad parenting creates messed up children, but why do dishonesty, criminality, and evil spread from this?" Will asked.

"That's an essential question. When you teach people to see the world as a hostile and dangerous place instead of giving them the tools to solve all their problems, you set them up for a follower mentality.[lxiii] They don't know how to protect themselves and invite scrupulous characters who exploit them rather than defending them. That is how the seeds of corruption are planted and grow into a garden of depravity."

As the two figures left the night park, Will saw Morgan's body fade away into nothingness as if a transporter had beamed him up. Will realized he was alone again and felt like he was the only person alive in the universe.

RULE OF PRINCIPLE 14: *Do not use religion or tradition as an excuse to abuse children. God is not on your side here. Hitting and beating children (& spouses) from anger is a form of violent abuse on the powerless.*

Reserve the use of spanking for times when all other options fail. Try other nonviolent forms of punishment instead. If age-appropriate, explain to children how this behavior adjustment and non-physical penalties will make them a happier, well-adjusted adult.

22. Night 8 - NOSTALGIA

He was driving down familiar roads, looking at the same landmarks that gave a sense of being part of the community. His hometown felt safe, even though he was one soul living among millions. Will's phone buzzed, and he picked it up to answer the telephone.

A glance at the screen revealed that it was Angel. What the hell? Should he answer it? Yes. He was anxious to have an intimate conversation with a beautiful woman. Why the hell not?

This civil engineer pulled his BMW smoothly over into an empty parking spot to allow the rest of the rush hour traffic to dart by and pressed the answer key.

Angel was in a shopping mall nearby, and she wanted to talk while sipping her evening latte. As the two former lovers began to chat about everything they could think of, they felt the familiar sensations of affection and nostalgia bubbling up from the deep past. They had shared some great times. Some enjoyable memories.

They had surprising moments of philosophical discussions on this call. Why are women so much better dancers than men? She wondered out loud.

He guessed. Maybe women are like bright flags, meant to flap and dance in the wind, while men are the flagpole.

Sturdy & tough so they can raise their partner to the sky. Content to let their partner receive the glory and attention.

I like that story, 'Mr. Stick in the Mud,' she said.

Will believed that there were still some unresolved issues that she wanted to talk about, but he did not want to ruin the opening chapter of this second chance. Talking about their relationship was their 'secret place', a maze of conversations that only they could co-create together. He had forgotten that the engine was running and finally turned off the ignition half an hour into the conversation.

Did he want to see her again? Without question. Although he was unaware of it, he had just begun a perilous path.

23. Construction - Businesses That Become Criminal Gangs Blur The Lie

The silhouette of a man stood in front of an empty construction site. As a civil engineer, Will knew what was going on at this simple three plex retail and office complex even though it belonged to a competitor's client. He had gotten many construction boots muddy walking through worksites and felt as comfortable outdoors as in his office.

Morgan appeared next to him, "Can't stay away from work, huh?"

"This is not our site. I'm just taking a break from my walk."

"Oh, I know. I also know you would rather be working than building a life of your own. If that project did not fall through, you would be at your desk right now."

Will could not disagree. It was true.

"Some observers believe that if you fall into the wrong industry, someone will inevitably corrupt you. I say that the groundwork for corruption happens in infancy, and your moral code can stop the hostile environment from turning you selfish and cruel."

"Babies are born innocent because they don't know better. But they are also selfish because they don't understand that there are other people in the world. They can't see the separation between themselves and the world around them. It's just their wants and needs."

"Good parents teach them to be considerate of others before heading to preschool. Later our culture unteaches them by making children agents of their profit or pleasure."

"Materialism causes people to become less considerate of others by persuading them to chase money and fun?" asked Will.

"You got it. When a culture like ours encourages personal consumption, we make workers represent their interests. They may find lying and deception practical servants in finding success, and they could spiral out of moral control in pursuit of endless pleasure.[lxiv]"

"Between the ages of four and six, children develop a sense of right and wrong. They learn about beliefs and values. Others have distinct personalities that conflict with them due to having different beliefs and values.[lxv] We learn lying becomes a technique to make people happier, to get things from them, and to avoid confrontation," said Morgan.

"So, how does lying make us more selfish and dishonest?"

"The cost of lying is a betrayal of trust. It's the loss of meaningful friendships. We lie to protect others' feelings and maybe avoid giving them additional worries, but we are doing it to avoid solving messy, uncomfortable problems."

"The problem is that our rational minds may accept the lie, but our intuition knows better than that. Subconsciously, people can tell when others are being deceitful and turn inward to protect themselves and their inner circle. Hence, selfishness flourishes."

"Even if we guard ourselves against cheating, why do some people become dishonest, and others adhere to an upright moral code?" asked Will.

"Excellent question. People are always watching others for clues and then making moral judgments based on what emotions drive them the most."

"Take construction and contractors. Construction is a desirable industry for dishonest people to make substantial money because huge cash sums have to trade hands to buy land, materials, and labor every day. It's very tempting to cheat because business is on the honor system. A builder's reputation is critical."

"When contractors have long term thinking, strong ties to the community, an infinity to God, they will have little incentive to cheat provided they are honest souls. Contractors with short term thinking, are transient, and have overwhelming pressure to satisfy their desires, addictions, and compulsions have fewer reasons to be reliable."

"Great tip. Now I know what to look out for when hiring a tradesperson or builder."

"This applies to any type of financial deal. Whether buying a business, hiring a lawyer, finding a wedding planner, you should always look for signs of high moral character."

"Getting back to contractors. Some managers will sell land, trucks, concrete, and building supplies at inflated prices and kick back some money to the buyer under the table. Other developers will flip buildings at overpriced valuations, and the estimators, real estate agents, and sellers will get big paydays. The buyer will continue this cycle because he or she will do the same thing when he sells property again."

"Does this dirty and hard industry become corrupted because they get workers from the margins of society like parolees, criminals, and new immigrants?"

"One of many causes, employers have difficulty finding enough laborers, and many men leaving prison can't find good solid work due to their reputation. They join construction crews and see what dirty stuff is going on."

"The clever ones abandon street crime like car thefts and break-ins and try to get into bigger stuff like smuggling, drug deals, and money laundry. Dirty money from drugs and crime can be funneled into construction products and then returned clean when they sell buildings."

"Some petty criminals use home sites to scan for prospective break-ins, carjacking, or just pocket valuables while walking through rooms. If the homeowner or building manager is not aware of it, drug trades, prostitution, and other criminal transactions can take place on construction sites."

"That is so interesting. I just thought the homebuyer had to worry about paying for inferior quality, but there is so much more to it." Will admitted his naivety.

"Many businesses are not criminal in nature, but they provide dishonest services. Some contractors promise to do a great job and then fail to complete the work once they get the deposit. More than a few companies start with inexpensive repairs and then 'con' up additional construction work soaking the poor homeowner with unnecessary projects."

"And everything starts with lying to deceive the victim. That is why you don't like deception," Will asked.

"Here is another theory. The only reason criminals have a hope and prayer of success in their betrayal is that the vast majority of people act from a code of decency and honor. This space of trust is where cons come in and violate it. When everyone turns dishonest, the credit, labor, housing, manufacturing markets will all grind to a halt because deals can't happen without trust."

"Well, can you confirm that?" he asked.

Morgan backed away from the fence and shrugged his shoulders. "It seems so. Picture the level of trust and kindness inside a prison, among inmates, and you can see how eroding ethical standards in the business world can make life tougher for everyone."

RULE OF PRINCIPLE 15: *Please don't steal from others or engage in unethical business practices. Criminals are often not happy people. They can't trust their associates. They are on edge and worried about getting robbed themselves, and so money comes and goes. Stealing and cheating may give them pleasure but not lasting happiness. The riches of the sinful lifestyle are not worth the risk or costs.*

24. Money Laundering - Mind The Grey Area Between Dishonesty & Honesty

"It's a myth that star athletes, math geniuses, concert pianists, or violent criminals were born that way. Guardians nurture their innate talents and help them grow into who they are to become."

"Um, are you saying an NFL player and a bank robber are taught to do what they do once they showed interest in that particular activity," asked Will.

"Yes, we all have some seed of greatness inside us right inside our dark side. The darkness consumes some, and failures never discover the gifts given to them."

"If you put a child in enough pain, he or she will act out of pure self-interest without regard to anyone else. In some neighborhoods, children see the shadow everywhere and in every person. Suspicion becomes selfishness, greed, rage, and hate. Evil and destruction become normalized."

"That explains the crook's behavior. What about the football player?

"His evil shadow is sitting in the background, underutilized, waiting. The athlete may never do anything that brings it out because his mind is focused on winning games, practicing, doing endorsement deals, and charity events. His life is too rich and full to cause trouble for others."

"That is crazy, man. It's like we have an evil switch in us that others turn on, so we shift into violence and dishonesty," said Will

"Your on/off switch can't just be flicked on and off like a light. It takes months and years for a person to build up their criminal tendencies."

"Criminals do not just break the law because it's in their nature, and they do not stomp all over others impulsively. No, they are aware of the environment they are in and are alert to cues or signs that it is safe to commit crimes."

"When institutions and communities fall apart, trash appears on the ground and graffiti on the walls; it's a signal that owners are mismanaging wealth and property. Eroding standards are also a welcome mat to dishonest people to try to see how they can steal and cheat others in the area[lxvi]."

"I have a feeling you want to talk about unusual forms of criminality," said Will

"Oh, you have heard of this one. Money laundering is a crime of sophistication that requires the integration of legal institutions like banks and law firms with underworld organizations like the Mafia or Chinese gangs."

"When the average person thinks about criminality, they think about drug deals, carjacking, muggers, and home robberies. Street crime is not where gangs make fortunes.

Employee fraud and theft is ten times greater in sheer dollars than the total income of all robberies."

"The amount of tax cheating in the US at six to nine hundred billion dollars is much higher than all street crime. Lucrative crime can take place inside of offices and boardrooms, not merely in back alleys or parking lots."

"That blows my mind," Will admitted.

"What happens to all that money from the sale of slaves, prostitution, gambling, illegal drug & alcohol, and black-market activities? The brightest people with dark leanings are recruited to learn how to take their banking, accounting, and legal knowledge and move dirty money across borders and transform it into untraceable legitimate currency."

"Depravity steals money away from legitimate & honest businesses and drives it underground where other criminals provide other dirty & unregulated services."

The demand for illegal drugs, gambling, and prostitution increases when rich folks need to hide their ill-gotten gains. Money laundering involves massive dollar amounts, so when these bankers and businessmen buy, they favor luxury homes, clothing, cars, boats, jewelry, art, planes, and other forms of excess."

Will asked, "I am lost again. How does this white-collar crime hurt ordinary people?"

"Our dark side is embarrassing to us. We try to suppress it and hide it from others, but it leaks out in ways we can't predict. Most of us would not dream of using a gun to rob a passerby yet walking into a bank with a suitcase of dirty money to launder it for another businessman? That is something we can rationalize. There is no mask and no gun. Just us in a suit sitting across from a shady banker in a bank office. It's almost mundane and routine."

"When you mix a legitimate business activity like banking with something criminal, like moving gang money, it creates a conflicting picture in our heads. We know it is wrong, yet it does not feel as wrong as violent crime. We bank all the time. Maybe we have helped someone illiterate or infirm with their banking."

"This grey area of corruption looks wonderful to those who exploit circumstances to gain advantage rather than being guided by consistent principles. It allows risk-averse criminals to break the law only if it's perfectly safe to do so."

"So money-laundry and smuggling can be the gateway drug to other forms of fraud and criminality?" asked Will.

"Mostly, no. Fraudsters can enjoy a luxurious lifestyle through these transactions and still appear to be upstanding society members. Participating in church activities and charity work helps suppress feelings of guilt or shame."

"Are you now seeing me connect the dots? How we could corrupt every aspect of life if we allow our darker impulses to dominate our thoughts?"

Will started to walk away from the construction site, back home. "Yeah, I get it. I wish we could talk about something more pleasant, but you have opened up my eyes to a part of life I could not see before."

Morgan matched his pace and blocked Will from proceeding once they reached the corner. "We all wish to live in a land of rainbows and lollipops, but that is just not the cruel reality of life."

"Have a good night."

"Bye, Morgan" They shook hands and walked in opposite directions.

RULE OF PRINCIPLE 16: *Aiding criminals within legitimate businesses is also unethical but hard to circumvent. Please avoid attracting or marketing to this element. White-collar criminals are not as frightening to the public as street thugs and seldom receive harsh criticism, judgment, or fines in proportion to their crimes.*

Set fair and just penalties for rule-breakers and then be consistent in their application. White-collar criminals do not receive as punishing sentences as blue-collar criminals, nor do police forces invest as many resources in arresting these gangs. This injustice contributes to the moral decline of our society.

25. Night 9 - MAGIC

Their chemistry was palatable to anyone passing by. Will and Angel could not keep their hands off each other after leaving the restaurant. A few gawkers looked on in envy as the attractive couple embraced each other, leaning against his BMW. The magnetism between them was thick and vibrant; they were fighting to control their deepest urges.

Will flirtatiously suggested that they should head over to her place. Angel teased that they would have more fun sooner if they went to his apartment.

He never drove home so fast. Will decided to forget about the past. The sleepless nights. The tense arguments. The long silences. Angel ran her hands along his pant leg as if to hint what was to come.

It was her curves, the lines of her body that Will wanted to touch. She desired to press her face against his hairy, firm chest, and if he let her squeeze the muscles in his arms and legs, she would allow him to run his hands over her body.

They disappeared into Will's apartment and shut the door.

26. Food Industry - Global Brands Desire Addiction Until Your First Heart Attack

Will was still glowing with memories of the night before. A turn of the key in the door to his apartment, and he bounded in, full of energy. Morgan was already there, looking through the refrigerator door at the contents inside.

"Hey, it looks like you need to go shopping for groceries soon. Never saw a sadder collection of leftovers and stale veggies in a bachelor's pad."

"Could you give me more warning next time? Maybe call ahead?" complained Will.

"I don't have a phone, and I have no more control over our encounters than you do."

"Speaking of establishing warnings and rules. Do you know how to train a dog or cat?" asked Morgan suddenly.

"Mmm, you make your dog repeat the trick over and over. When your pet completes the desired behavior, you give your dog a tasty treat as a reward. If the pet acts up or disobeys, you withhold the treat until it does what you want. I think that's right?" pondered Will.

"Yeah, that is how most people train their pets. Do you think human children can be trained in a similar way to behave?"

Will speculated: "Oh, that does seem like one way we teach our children how to behave, except..."

"Would you entertain the possibility that the dark and manipulative shadowy side of food manufacturer executives devised many such strategies to insert their sugary and salty offerings into the parenting strategies of modern society?

"What! No. That's unbelievable. Not likely," argued Will.

"You need a history lesson, Will. The combination of branding, television, and supermarketing advertising helped a few factories grow into multinational corporate giants. As the competition dropped off, and these companies consolidated their hold on the food industry, they became even more hungry for growth and profits."

"Since regulation and oversight have weakened in the past fifty years, firms began to remove the natural, nutritious ingredients and replace it with cheaper components like salt, sugar, corn & wheat. Businesses employ scientific researchers to find out how to make these foods extremely addictive and affordable[lxvii]."

"Many multinational companies looked at ways to create products just for children with colorful characters and cartoons that looked like television programs. Marketers trained kids as young as two to emotionally attach to the food product's character by presenting them as fun and heroic."

"When families went shopping for groceries, young and old felt compelled to buy the branded cookies, ice cream, soft drinks, or cereal even though there were infinite affordable and nutritious alternatives available."

"The convenience of finger foods and microwavable meals filled with sugar and salt has led to a culture of overweight and unhealthy consumers. European governments have much tighter controls over advertising and ingredients, but in North America, governments don't enforce restrictions well, all in the name of commerce and jobs."

"Wait, go back to that dog training story and how food manufacturers took control over our eating habits. What is the psychology of this manipulation?" asked Will.

"When threats, like withholding snacks, and bribes like cookies, are used to control behavior, children learn to display good behavior for rewards. They also hide poor activities to avoid punishment.[lxviii] Praise from a parent is linked to the sugar, fat, and salt in snack foods and trains children to associate the pleasant tastes to their childhood's warm memories."

"As the children grow up, their taste buds become habituated to desire only manufactured salty and sugary foods and reject the blander, natural sweetness, and texture of fruits and vegetables. If you win children over early, they get hooked for life."

"After parental influences are gone, and young adults get to make their own life choices, they will reach for foods and brands associated with their childhood. Conditioning is part of the reason it's challenging to change our eating habits. It's psychological triggers that make us eat the wrong foods, not just smell, colors, taste, and texture.

"And then when I am stressed, angry, bored, or depressed, I reach for my favorite snacks to push down all the negative feelings of my dark side."

"Food manufacturers also manipulate our behaviors by placing their snacks and products everywhere so that it is extremely convenient to purchase and difficult to avoid. Since this is low-quality nourishment with high-profit margins, food brands pay supermarkets and gas stations extra incentives to stock their brand over others. The fruit and vegetable farmers and lobby groups do not have such bags of money to compete."

"I can see this unethical, but it's not illegal."

"That's because the food manufacturing lobby rigs the system so they can conduct business as they see fit. If the government had the public's interest at heart, they would teach nutrition, restrict advertising towards children, control the amount of sugar and salt in products, and generally support organic & locally sourced greens rather than subsidize beef, corn, and wheat."

"Society encourages the consumption of processed foods because it's easier and more profitable to produce. The human costs are horrific but are postponed far into the future; we can't see how much we lose in such a bargain."

"It is too complex a subject to discuss how heart disease, obesity, diabetes and fatigue from a poor diet contributes to poor sleep, inattentiveness, lack of focus, memory loss, shorter lives, depression, anxiety, and worry?[lxix] Are these destructive forces enough to raise your sense of indecency from mild to outrage?" asked Morgan.

"I am too tired to argue," Will said. He left the kitchen and flopped onto his back on the sofa. He looked at his hallucination expectantly for hints where the conversation was going next.

"You were a busy boy last night, huh?" Morgan teased Will. "Younger and thinner consumers make fun of overweight folks out of ignorance of all the forces that trap them into overeating. Our dark side enjoys beating up the victims of unethical activities because we celebrate in relief that we escaped the attack ourselves."

"Don't be so quick to judge those who have bulging waistlines. Mocking fat people does not solve any of your problems and degrades your character. Do you see the ugliness in others that you can't face yourself when you look in the mirror? Maybe you could lose a few pounds yourself?"

RULE OF PRINCIPLE 17: *Would you believe you are in an abusive relationship with food companies marketing happiness but encouraging unhealthy lifestyles? Don't trust firms that manufacture food as addictive as cocaine because they are not legally responsible for your heart disease, cancer, or diabetes. Instead, search for independents & health stores*

Have compassion for those who are failing or struggling. Obesity may not reflect a lack of willpower but part of living in a society surrounded by plentiful food and characters who feed this addiction at every turn. It's not 100% your fault you are overweight. (However, you must take responsibility for your health no matter what.)

27. Government Debt - If You Don't Protest, Grandchildren Will Foot The Bill

Morgan left the kitchen and leaned against the bookcase near the sofa. He looked down at Will's shoes, partially off his feet, dangling off the armrest.

"Did you know that overweight people are also very likely to owe a significant amount of personal debt? They are symptoms of the same problem - overconsumption today with a failure to recognize the costs of postponing the pain until tomorrow."

"Politicians and legislators in government do not want to accept responsibility for their behavior because they rarely pay for the consequences at the polls. That is why government spending has gotten out of control, and national, state & city debts have grown tenfold in the past forty years."

"Younger politicians have become addicted to using debt as an escape card to avoid making discerning austerity measures to balance their annual budgets. The older generation had tougher attitudes about debt because they would only spend those tax dollars collected. Seniors would not borrow unless necessary."

"That's kind of unfair. My grandparents' generation got us into multiple wars while this crop fights for human rights and improving the health and well-being of all. We have different priorities." protested Will.

"Of course, each generation has its attributes and flaws. You make a good point. Let us not fall into the trap of claiming the older generations are superior to their children. Not true. Each person and age manifests their dark side in unique ways that indicate the time and place they grew up in."

"No matter what generation, children learn to lie from their parents. They see their parents lie to neighbors or the police to avoid trouble. Kids observe lying in adults who try to avoid hurting the feelings of others[lxx]. Teenagers learn to lie about rebellious acts like dating, wasting time, and drinking alcohol."

"Parents also collude in this deception, partly because they don't want to know about certain indiscretions of their children's lives.

"You speak of frequently lying in as many nights as I can remember. Why is this so?" probed Will.

"Lying is the fundamental building block of deception, cheating, stealing, fraud, and all types of criminality and dishonest behavior...Were you not paying attention to what I said the first couple of nights?"

"Everyone persuades - some are much more skilled at it than others. Too many politicians have the skill to deceive by making false promises and also have a weak sense of character that prevents them from standing by difficult decisions. That is how government budgets can get out of control."

"We know that if your family spends more money than you earn, you need to borrow that money and pay it back. If you don't pay it back, someone will seize your car, home, or ruin your credit rating."

"What if governments borrow billions of dollars to pay for spending today that taxpayers of the future will have to pay for long after they are retired and dead?"

"These politicians are stealing resources from the future to relieve today's taxpayers' anxieties, worries, and greed," stated Will.

"You got that right. The consequences of this action are more dreadful than you might believe."

"I am an engineer. This is not in my wheelhouse," stated Will.

"Your dark side uses many types of techniques to avoid difficult issues that need attention. When you feel boredom, anger, fear, or procrastination coming on, your feelings give you a way out. By letting wounds fester, your future is going to be full of out of control anxiety, worry, and frustration when problems at your doorstep force you to act.[lxxi]"

"Do you understand that government debt means much higher taxes in the future? It implies massive spending cuts when the lenders or bondholders of government debt come collecting.[lxxii] Nations could go bankrupt and start selling buildings & land to pay off the creditors. That means unpaid bills, crumbling roads, unsafe bridges, fewer inspectors, fewer nurses and teachers, shuttered schools, and hospitals."

"Like when my ex-wife and I charged up to $5,400 in credit card fees for a Las Vegas vacation? Then I had four lean months where I put all my spare cash into my credit card account to pay it down," said Will.

"That is what a responsible family does with debt. Vague concepts like federal or state debt and spending shortfalls do not trigger an emotional response to the way personal debt does. Hence, taxpayers allow politicians to take the path of least resistance."

"Almost every country in the world is increasing their debts faster than is financially prudent, and it could become a global crisis that will make the Great Depression of the 1930s look like a tea party,"

"When the debt comes due, and taxpayers, including businesses, are asked to start paying higher taxes, these corporations will either be sold off, merged, bankrupt, or move to tax-havens. The middle-class taxpayers of future generations will probably end up paying far higher income taxes than those who benefited from this financial stupidity!"

"This seems more like an economics issue. Why should I care?" asked Will.

"When governments raise taxes to pay for old debts, families get squeezed, and they can't afford to manage their household bills. Taxpayers justify this betrayal with their tax cheating, lying, and deceiving of the tax revenue department. Do you realize that lying about debt destroys trust between governments and taxpayers?"

"The growth of underground black markets means even more deceit and deception between customers and suppliers because there is no moral authority to oversee such transactions."

"When citizens no longer trust the government or free market, they view their suppliers and customers with suspicion and demand harsher terms. Unstable companies cannot qualify for the credit, and then businesses fear to hire new employees. Innovations slow down. Children can't afford college, and builders can't find qualifying homebuyers. Would you like to live in such a hostile environment?"

"Fine. That sounds so horrible I don't want to hear anymore. Now get out," Will commanded.

"Your wish is my command." Morgan disappeared like switching off a television. Will immediately felt guilty for being rude but then reminded himself Morgan was not a real person. Why did he teach such awful subjects? Was it okay to argue with his subconscious? He was not sure.

RULE OF PRINCIPLE 18: *If you take care of your neighbor, he will want to care about you. Government debt is a violation of the golden rule, which requests we treat people as kindly as possible. Unethically, we pass the buck to others, and they relinquish it on to future generations. Screw them, right? Wrong. Humans of today are paying for the sins of previous generations a hundred years ago.*

Assign the people you know as nicely as the treatment you desire for yourself. Moral citizens will also act to protect future generations' interests because such guardianship causes the evolution of ethics into something mystic.

28. Night 10 - SHOOTER

Will and Mike, an old friend from high school, dropped into the gun emporium. The Glock was ready. Mike was more excited than Will about the new gun. He examined it from all angles and fingered the bullets as if made of solid gold.

Where can they practice firing this thing? In the back. The back of the store had a five-lane shooting range. It used to be an old bowling alley, but when the regular bowlers died out, the landlords sold out, and the new owners had placed target practice figures at the end of the old bowling lanes.

Mike did not have a shooter of his own, so he rented one for an hour of gunfire. Most of the seven players occupying the four lanes appeared to be confident at handling their weapons.

Neither man could shoot a lick. Mike was marginally better than Will, but if they did manage to hit the bullseye marks, it was purely by accident than by design.

Die Mother&#% die! he screamed in his head as the bullets rang true. Will felt like the harbinger of death and the bringer of destruction. He felt amazing.

Unfortunately, his confidence did not result in inaccuracy. The closest he got to the bullseye was the outer ring of the target practice sheet. His forty-two attempts at firing his gun resulted in sixteen hits on the target and twenty-six misses.

Mike hit twenty-nine strikes out of forty one-shots on his target.

Better keep practicing. Mike laughed at Will. Your shooting stinks; you will probably blast off your foot before hitting anyone else, he teased.

29. Veterans & Retirees - Remember The Past Or Risk Destroying The Future

Another sleepless night. Who in their right mind would visit a war memorial in the wee hours of the night? Will. That's who. He was one more loser who felt out of place in a world that was churning along without him.

"Hi, Morgan, you crazy old ghost. Here to keep me company?"

"Hello, Will. Why not?"

Morgan had appeared from behind the statue and was approaching with his hand extended in friendship.

"I'm no ghost. You know that."

"It would be easier to take if you were a ghost rather than a conjuring of my mind. At least then, I would not be losing my mind," said Will.

"You are as sane as everyone else, Will. Just go with it and you will see better things when I am gone. If you can focus, we are talking about winners and losers in this capitalist game."

"The rich and powerful learn how to win the old games of commerce and politics and then rewrite these rules for their offspring can win too. One of these rules or beliefs is that business success is a meritocracy. Anyone may participate freely, and those with the greatest skills and work ethic usually win this game[lxxiii]."

"Of course, the real world is not as advertised. Those with access to capital, the right connections, and preferred skin color & gender usually get much further than smarter, hungrier competitors who don't. Your socio-economic group counts because if you live among the wealthy, customers can pay more, and banks will lend more."

"Nevertheless, most Americans believe in this concept of meritocracy. This unfounded faith in work fairness brings out our harshness against those who do poorly financially. If they are broke & lack homes, cars, or businesses, it must mean they are lazy or foolish[lxxiv]. No other alternate ideas may entertain our minds when we have a fixed mindset toward this belief."

"We seem to have this overly enthusiastic admiration and joy in the young, the new, and the fresh. Full of potential & promise, we love to see the births, young adults getting married, children graduating from high school, and grown-ups entering the field as new accountants, doctors, lawyers, and other professionals.

"But we also dislike the old, the broken, and the familiar. When things don't work, we quickly abandon it before anyone notices and starts something else. The dark side of us hates losers. We feel surges of negative emotions when our sports team loses, or if we fail in the dating arena, or observe friends go bankrupt."

"Many of the last thirty years' failed parenting strategies are making a mockery of the old meritocracy because some children receive faulty skills to join the workforce.[lxxv] Children need unconditional love and acceptance, but they are not getting enough from absent parents and don't get it from other youngsters either."

"Kids spend time with peers who value them for their humor, athletic skills, cultural awareness, coolness, or rebelliousness. This need to be held in high regard suggests that children with absent or permissive parents will avoid learning difficult skills where they might look incompetent. They choose to play socially acceptable pastimes like video games, sports, and musical instruments."

"This cultural development takes millions of children out of running. They simply don't have the skills to compete."

"When adults neglect children, kids may not have the grit and resilience to try over and over again. It's highly likely some will become nihilistic, angry, and pessimistic in the process."

"Many develop self-pity and act like victims needing rescuing. Observing weakness triggers the darkest emotional sense of unfairness and resentment to those 'winners' who solved their problems through unassisted struggle and daring. The victims of this system disagree, believing life has screwed them, and someone is to blame."

"We find it offensive that losers in this system would ask for help or pity. Complainers and whiners feel childish to us. We demand that adults shut up and figure out their problems.[lxxvi]"

"On the other hand, once that hard-working worker retires, the powerful athlete becomes disabled, that brave soldier comes home limping and broken, we no longer care. The proof is in how little press and advertisements they receive. You don't see many ads with seniors or overweight or disabled people selling toothpaste or cars or snack food. We like youthful energy and not frail mortals, who ran out of time."

"We also display our thoughtlessness and lack of investment in their well being in the skimpy pensions they receive or the lack of government programs & funding for disabled citizens and war veterans."

"As a result, war veterans do not demand the medical services they deserve or the pensions promised. Their guilt for letting themselves get injured, older, and reliant on the government is embarrassing to their sense of independence."

"The irony is too much to bear. Those citizens who believed the most in loyalty to country, pride in the armed forces, and hometown fidelity are discarded and forgotten, hidden away in nursing homes and public hospitals. Cast aside because they fought on the losing side. Or maybe they won by but outlived their usefulness. Who knows?"

"It's like their shortcomings are reminders of our failings, and in a world where we only want to win, we prefer to show our best side to our competition. We have decided to reject and hide the aging, decay, death, and destruction of our greatest warriors. Our dark side cannot tolerate ugliness and thus makes us uglier than that we despise."

RULE OF PRINCIPLE 19: *Ethical people can observe good behavior in others and prefer to surround themselves with moral characters. The more goodness around you, the healthier you are to resist malicious personalities. Learn to judge people by their actions and not by their gender, nationality, age, sexual preference, religion, or race. To do so would be hypocritical because you will favor weaker players of your own tribe whom you prefer.*

30. Banking - Avoid Consumer Debt Or You Could Be Trapped For Life

"All humans are inconsistent when they order or request others to do things that they won't do themselves. Maybe they prohibit followers' behavior that they sometimes indulge in themselves. Some call that hypocrisy. I call it fantastical & aspirational thinking that makes people desire unrealistic situations that are impossible to sustain."

"And this part of the battle between the dark and light wolves?" Will asked.

"Ah, yes. It's the constant battle between the dark side and its brother, the light. Sometimes the light wins, and you perform kind deeds, do what you say you would, and stay until finished. Occasionally the shadow wins, and you act lazy, lie irresponsibly, and even cheat others. Inconsistency creates a lack of trust and respect among hypocritical families & societies."

"Parents send mixed messages to their children. In some circles, children may receive the cultural message that they have the same rights and privileges as their parents[lxxvii]. Parents may also reverse leadership roles and ask the kids to make major decisions that they are not ready to make."

"This confuses children who grow to believe they have the authority in the relationship and do not need to consult with adults over difficult decisions. Inevitably, they grow up into adults who make foolish money decisions once they get their first credit card & job."

"So the children are bewildered about when to listen to their parents and when to rebel?" asked Will.

"Young children do not have the experience and wisdom to make good and consistent decisions. Until they reach late teens, they are impulsive and unrefined. Their behaviors are short-sighted, emotional, and irrational because they are still learning to attain social skills, language, and scientific nuance[lxxviii]."

"The inexperienced will view the game of finance & banking completely differently than the expert who has learned from his mistakes. Multiply these different events and skills with the hundreds of different roles in life, and you can see how a, say, thirty-year-old adult thinks completely differently than a sixteen-year-old."

"If children don't receive the guidance they needed from the start, they begin to make bad financial decisions as adults?"

."Financial institutions can easily manipulate consumers if clients don't learn how to research, make decisions, and protect themselves from risk.[lxxix] Some children grow up to become financially cautious, and every banking decision is a worrisome catastrophe that they would rather avoid. Paying it safe is a losing proposition because they will avoid investments that can win them financial freedom

"Other children are far too overconfident. They are rash and aggressive in their borrowing and investing because they grew up with lots of positive reinforcement from admirers & friends and very little advice from responsible adults[lxxx]. Amateurs seem to have distorted views of how to measure the risks and rewards of finances."

"Financially uneducated, young consumers fresh out of school, many looking to buy a house, get married, and start families have no idea how to handle money. Credit cards eventually get charged to the maximum limit."

"Yes, they buy lots of nice clothes, dinners out, speedboats, and furniture without realizing that this debt at twenty percent interest will require a large portion of our future income to pay off," said Will.

"And when they lose their jobs or have a financial disaster, they can't manage their finances as well as debt-free households. Reputations are misaligned, and self-esteem is damaged when debtors' bank accounts no longer reflect their desired goals."

"Many treat the broke and bankrupt very harshly, but that is their dark side judging that what they fear about themselves. Some couples plan clever financial strategies, but bills can drain wealth to nothing if one partner gets very sick or loses their job. The family finds there are more unavoidable expenses than income to sustain their bank balances."

"Employees who assign up to half their income to service their creditors find it difficult to change their station in life. They can't move to other cities or seek further education, choose more desirable investments or start healthier jobs because they have to work enough hours to pay off debts that are consuming their worries and thoughts[lxxxi]."

"It is in the interest of the banking industry to put consumers into credit card, business, and mortgage debt. Not so much that customers struggle to pay off debt, but enough that banks can maximize profits. Banking institutions do not want educated customers who know how to borrow money and pay it off quickly because that means slower growth & smaller profit."

"Where banking institutions lend money freely, the wealthy use it to accumulate investments that make them even richer. In contrast, the poor use debt for entertainment and buying things that lose their value."

"You are saying that banks are being irresponsible by offering customers far more credit than is advisable, trapping them into a lifetime of debt servicing? That is hypocrisy, is it not?"

"Of course. Banks used to be the guardians of other peoples' wealth. Now they are exploiting our dark side's greedy inclination to consume by transferring money from their customers into their coffers in the form of interest payments."

"I think you can see when a small group of capitalists builds extreme wealth from the labors of the overworked majority; it raises the question of morality, decency, and injustice. Taken to extremes, this is how societies crumble, and revolutionary wars ignite."

"Marxism has proven to be a failure, but unbridled capitalism is also punishing its supporters. We need a third option quickly."

"It's a bit tiring to talk about such things, so let's quit here. Later, Will."

Morgan walked off into the distance at the edge of the park. Will called out after him, "Hey, how can you get tired if you are my hallucination? Come on. I still don't feel like sleeping. Let's keep going..."

RULE OF PRINCIPLE 20: *Avoid paying your credit cards or loans, and you will lose in hundreds of ways unimaginable. Always pay off your debts (unless it's impossible to do so). Debts are an obligation that a person of character agrees to hold to and complete to the end—accepting bankruptcy when avoidable is a form of stealing.*

Other consumers pay for bad loans, not finance companies. To obtain money from other working people is unkind. Even worse, if you are dishonest here, you lose trust in yourself and others. You may quit beneficial projects, courses, and jobs because your identity is that of a quitter.

31. Night 11 - CONFUSION

Will was thinking about her just about every minute of the day. Man, he wanted to call her badly. Was it worth making the call? No, he would come across as needy, he thought.

As he started to text her, he changed his mind and gave her a ring. She answered right away. He sat down, cross-legged on the bed to have a long conversation. Angel muffled the receiver with her hand. She jumped in mid-sentence as Will started to talk about the billing on his insurance claim, apologized, and hung up abruptly. Will stared at his phone in surprise. He hit the redial button, but the call went to voicemail.

He then remembered she hated talking about money. Many of their fights eventually ended up on the topic. Will regretted accusing her multiple times of desiring a richer boyfriend when they began to have divergent opinions about their future together.

Angel furiously shook at being labeled a gold digger; she thought dumping her wealthy gentlemen suitors for him was proof enough. Why did men always assume more money would solve all their problems?

If this couple had fought about money, it was a disagreement about how much was enough and what they were willing to sacrifice to get it. The boyfriend wanted to work incredibly hard to accumulate a pile of it so they could have a dream car, house, and wedding. The girlfriend wanted to be comfortable enough to live modestly and use their salaries to have endless weekend adventures together.

'What about her huge wardrobe and jewelry?' he questioned her years ago. It would take big paychecks to keep her looking that good. She battled back with her take, 'people give me pretty things because it looks good on them to have me around. I don't need much to be happy. I hate that you think I am that kind of girl.'

He texted her to ask if anything was wrong. Forty minutes passed before she replied. Everything was fine. There were just unforeseen interruptions that she had to take care of tonight.

Both of them were lying in their beds, under the covers, engaging with each other. Sometimes the conversation was frantic, fast, and loud, and Will loved Angel's energy and enthusiasm. He much preferred when they talked slowly and quietly about nothing in particular.

Tonight was one of those nights. As minutes & hours whiled away, they sought the meandering lifeline of connection rather than being codependent playthings of pleasure.

It was nearly one in the morning when they finished messaging with each other. This indulgence was a mistake. The lovers had work in the morning—nevertheless, a lovely mistake.

32. Family Values - Employers Shouldn't Obstruct Parenting & Citizenship Duties

Will's heart was racing with excitement as he tossed and tumbled into a new dream.

Morgan appeared in front of him. The figure was blocking Will's view, so he stepped to the right, and Will could see the environment around him.

They were standing in a gorgeous, spacious living room in what must have been an enormously expensive house. The father was seen through the kitchen door, preparing dinner; the mother was at the dining table using a laptop while two children watched television. In their late thirties, the parents were still dressed up in suits and looking harried, as they had just come home after a long day at the office. The family could not see the intruders in their midst and carried on as if Will & Morgan were not there.

Morgan stood quietly observing this handsome family and then began speaking: "This house does not realize that they share the same human condition as everyone else. Two opposite pulls in conflicting directions simultaneously."

"One force, the light, is expansive and wants to grow, learn, and promote everyone's well-being in its orbit. The other energy is dark, contracting, protective, conservative, and unintentionally hurting those around it."

"You may be out of control of the environment that is forcing you towards the dark side. But you are completely the master of your values and beliefs, no matter how chaotic your life is·

Will asked, "You mean I can choose my character regardless of the circumstances around me?"

"Yes, you can choose to be a person of integrity and high skill even if you are in a culture that encourages deceit or laziness. Unfortunately, most people will take the easy route because doing hard things means questioning core beliefs about how the world works."

"If you question a heart belief about how the world works, your old identity may crumble. When adults do that, foolish friends mock them for having a midlife crisis. That is why we rarely question our childhood values."

"For example, you may believe these three cliches: marriage means constant fighting, that life is a struggle, or a good job will solve all your problems. Is this true? Humans prefer not to know, to stay congruent to core beliefs by pushing away contrary ideas."

"An essence belief of many people is that if they achieve wealth, fame, popularity, beauty, and power, they will become the center of attention, and this will make them feel content and secure."

"We know better. Popular people can become dependent on others' approval. If there is any withdrawal of praise, affection, power, and money by the social circle, their world could shake and break. Celebrities have become despondent and developed addictive behaviors when they fear a fall from grace. After all, the public determines their value, not them. Were you aware that chasing such a life puts high-status personalities in such a vulnerable position?"

"Are you going to talk about celebrities and popularity?" Will asked.

"No. Superficial status-seeking is just one of the whips of the hard work ethic and is one of many reasons why we neglect many non-work roles in the home, school, church, and sports arena."

"Many do not see fifty to seventy-hour workweeks as an immoral thing. What if this employment was not a choice but a form of entrapment and coercion? When workers put in more and more hours for less and less pay, they sacrifice everything else immeasurable in their lives - children, spouses, sleep, friends, exercise, church, hobbies, civic duties, volunteering. Everything!"

"Multinational corporations have soundly beaten down labor in the battle over hours, benefits, wages, and working conditions. In America, workers are not entitled to much sick pay or maternity leave, or can be fired for almost any reason because US governments have given businesses most of the power over employment."

Companies are free to hire and layoff workers as they please. Yes, there are worker protection rights, but managers write contracts to subvert its purpose. Big retail and restaurant chains keep many workers on call, so they have to wait for shifts and forgo lost wages if there is no full schedule."

"As a result, numerous young workers have postponed getting married and having children. Low wages, shift work, or lucrative careers with very long hours stretching into the evenings are two reasons for this delay. When companies don't pay adequate wages, workers often have to work overtime or work on weekends/evenings in two or more jobs to pay for necessities[lxxxii]. "

"With such workloads, families, hobbies, and community activities are neglected, and workers let some of their romantic relationships and friendships wither and die."

"That kind of sounds like my life. Except I have a great pension and health plan," said Will.

"You are rationalizing again. Your salary includes pensions, health packages, and other perks as a total package. You earned it. It's not a gift. Are you saying you love working harder and harder at the cost of your social life and potential for a new family?"

"When you put it that way...." Will said.

"Can you guess which life roles Americans define themselves best?"

"I am guessing that despite all the problems in the workplace, many people are more comfortable being at work than anywhere else?" Will guessed.

"True. The roles we play as a son, wife, daughter, husband, and grandparent are not as clearly defined as those at work. As we battle over who does what, we find it difficult to navigate family or community conflicts. On the other hand, our careers have fixed rules and expectations. We are praised for having certain job titles and for working consistent hours."

"Work culture is taking over North America. We were trained over twelve to sixteen or twenty years of school how to behave in the workplace. Very few people learn how to be parents, sons & daughters, friends, and lovers except through self-study and trial and error."

"As society continues to fragment, the knowledge required to cultivate relationships will continue to grow more complex. This role anxiety and instability are why many workers have unconsciously agreed to let work dominate their lives instead of confronting companies for more time with their families.

"It can't be that simple. There must be other factors or causes?" Will asked.

"Of course, there are dozens of other reasons like globalization, computerization, work at home projects, economic instability, and the rise and fall of new jobs and careers. Not to mention, increased migration patterns, governmental decline, 24-hour consumerism, declining spiritualism, smaller families, and much more."

"These are all symptoms, in any case. Traits of a culture that prioritized working to survive so far ahead of the family unit that the top one percent and all their supporters would rather work than learn how to become holistic and healthy human beings."

While he pondered this statement, Will and Morgan walked out of the living area and into the backyard garden. The sky was pitch black, but they could still see from the lumination of the kitchen windows. They sat down on the green patio lawn chairs and breathed in the night air.

RULE OF PRINCIPLE 21: *Work hard because the right career or calling can make you happy. Work hard to save for the future. Those are acceptable reasons. Working hard to climb the social ladder & show off is a mistake. The wealthy above you will look down at you in disdain for your lack, and jealous frienemies below you will look in envy for all you possess. There are no real winners in the status game. Only as a true friend can you have authentic relationships at all rungs of society.*

33. Materialism - Buy What You Need, Not What You Think You Want

"This is such a beautiful home. What a way to live." Will remarked.

"What a world we live in, to make such a place available for a select few. This wealthy English family probably has a very optimistic view of the world; after all, they have been rewarded very well for their hard work. Others are not as lucky for their efforts."

"Many, many people believe that society is going downhill because the narrative of the culture reinforces that stereotype[lxxxiii]. People watch the news, and the negative stories accumulate in our minds and age in a manner that makes us more cautious and fearful than we should be. Do you believe that to be true?" asked Morgan.

"You want me to say the world is getting better, right?" Will guessed.

"You assume wrong. Society is not getting better or worse, but our perception of the future is becoming pessimistic as technology feeds us increasingly threatening and perverse news stories."

"Whatever the culture you are born in, the types of stories, pictures, slang, and values are going to affect your own beliefs and behaviors considerably. The constant advertising attacks persuade audiences to have increased dissatisfaction with what they have. They start to envy what they are lacking and covet what their neighbors own."

"Yeah, I feel that way too. I always want more and get bored with what is sitting in my closet," contributed Will.

"These seductive ads are alluring and leading us to believe that purchasing more goods and services will give us more pleasure and happiness. But our incomes limit what we can buy, and we develop anger and resentment towards anyone we perceive is limiting our achievements."

"Oh my God, my coworkers complain about our boss every time he says no! I do that too," he said,

"In this consumer culture we have, we spend more time working, shopping, researching, and dreaming about the lifestyle we can't afford. Our families, spiritually, nature, hobbies, and communities are neglected because they are not as exciting or as beautiful as what is out there. And you know what happens when we ignore what we need for what we covet?"

"Our culture makes us more mentally ill? Maybe it makes us make bad decisions that are not in our interests?" said Will.

"I see you are slowly learning the truth. We develop internal conflicts about making the right decisions that should be easier to make, had we established our best priorities.

"Many no longer enjoy the simpler pleasures of walking, dancing, working, talking, and cooking because we believe we are losing out on the glamorous fun marketed to us. Some call it FOMO or 'fear of missing out,' I call FOMO as 'false objects marketed offensively.'"

"We can easily misinterpret the meaning of our choices. 'Fear of missing out' is a type of anxiety about making poor decisions. We waste much time doing things we would rather not do had we stayed true to our intuition."

"Only after decades of chasing, shopping, and consuming people realize that they wasted time buying false promises and worthless experiences that did not give them the satisfaction they craved[lxxxiv]."

"I understand that. Help me connect the dots. So how does that make people feed their dark side?" said Will.

"And we are back to the beginning. Humans need to hear things over and over until they get it. All disappointments or losses lead to frustration; frustration turns into anger; anger becomes hatred. Hatred makes us either destroy others or self-destruct our own constructed reality."

"Wow, you sound like Yoda. And then what happens?" Will asked.

"Bad stuff happens. People go against their true nature. For example, instead of going to school and building up their communities, youth sell drugs to buy material goods. They dehumanize their customers and other gang members. Then they shoot others encroaching on their territory. Now some are dead; others are in prison. The families are angry and attack the police."

"The police no longer go where they are not wanted, and the homes become nearly worthless. A culture of materialism can turn peaceful neighborhoods into hell for those who become mesmerized by its influence."

"That blows my mind. It's a good thing I live in a pretty nice area where cops do show up when they are needed," said Will.

"Remember, hell does not have a postal code. It's a state of mind for the living. Your neighbor, next door with the conforming car and branded clothes, could be living in his purgatory due to all his financial and personal troubles." smirked Morgan.

"Gary? Really. What trouble is he into?" asked Will.

"We are not here to gossip about your acquaintances, dumbass. You don't elevate yourself by being negative, cruel, or speaking ill of others. When a void lacking in love opens up, you are very likely to feed your dark side."

Morgan snapped his dirty fingers, and just like that, Will found himself in his bed. He opened his eyes and saw there was still no natural light coming through the windows. The alarm clock read 4: 42 AM. Another one and a half hours to get up, and Will was still bone-tired from a lack of sleep.

RULE OF PRINCIPLE 22 - *Do not trade in your good conscience for the opportunity for riches. Many are so desperate for the good life advertised to them dishonestly; they will engage in highly questionable activities to earn 'fun" money.*

Even if you gain material wealth from lying, stealing, and cheating others and avoid prison, there is always a cost to pay. Your integrity, reputation, self-worth, and peace of mind take a hit when you take advantage of people. Remember, if you are dishonest and your neighbors are crooked, co-operation & sharing are very difficult, and it's more painful for everyone to find the 'dream life.'

34. Night 12 - FRIGID

A lone man sat staring into nothingness on a park bench in the twilight of the evening. Strange behavior since most pedestrians rushed by on the sidewalk, clutching their gloves and coats, hurrying to get out of the frigid night air.

Will felt despondent. She was gone. He knew that chasing her with texts and calls would drive her away. Like most women, Angel liked to be pursued but not frantically by desperate suitors. His hallucination had warned him; sometimes, we can't stop ourselves from wrecking that we desire.

Or was his imagination playing tricks on him? Another smiley face text from Angel.

He was not in a mood for playing games. After the usual flirty & friendly greetings, he got serious. He fired off several texts asking what Angel wanted from him? Are they getting back together, or was he just another interlude between acts?

She replied that she didn't want to talk about that right now. There was a chance they could try again, but she wanted him to do something about it.

What did she want him to do? Angel could not put it into words. There hung a sense of frustration and confusion between the gaps in their correspondence.

Angel wrote a sweet goodnight message to Will, and they finished up for the night.

He realized that the protective warmth of his heavy winter coat was no longer protecting him. The wind was blowing up his trouser legs, and he was going to catch something bad if he stayed out any longer. Will got up off the bench and began to amble back to his apartment.

As Will reached to unlock the door of his apartment, a surprising message popped up on his screen. She must have felt compelled to share this revelation with him. Angel wrote that she wanted it all - marriage, children, careers, and her passions - if the fates told her to be with him, she would let him set the tone while she would take care of the details. What did that even mean?

35. Unions vs. Managers -Don't Gossip & Spread False Rumors

Will was on edge. He was pacing back and forth in his apartment. Anticipating more nights with his hallucinations was too much to take.

He knew that Morgan had told him that this would be over soon. He had his doubts. What if these visions never went away? What if he had Schizophrenia or something worse, and he was about to lose everything?

Will decided to go for a midnight drive. As he approached his BMW, he held his breath. Was Morgan inside the car? Good. Nobody was there.

As he adjusted the radio, he came across a familiar deep, soothing voice. Morgans' tenor voice came through the AM dial…

Will started to despair. Why won't you leave me alone? He thought it was cruel that he was suffering these delusions alone inside the darkest winter he had ever experienced.

Morgan recognized what the bleak expression on his student meant, "Don't fret, Will. You are undergoing a painful transformation that will be well worth the price once you emerge on the other side."

"We, humans, can't recognize what is extremely important and what is trivial unless someone reveals greater perspectives that reorient us to our true life mission. Do you not get caught up in silly gossip and rumors about our friends or enemies and fail to see that our era's politics and economics have completely undermined our emotional well being and financial peace of mind?"

"For example, political and corporate leaders have successfully portrayed union leaders as greedy, stubborn socialists blocking progress and prosperity for the rest of us, squeezing out small businesses to build a communist paradise. Lies. All lies."

"In truth, union groups have advocated for safer working conditions and helped create the modern middle class.[lxxxv] They are like sports agents who speak for all members and negotiate a better wage for all. They also fought to keep children out of the workplace, helped establish public schools, negotiated safety measures, and demanded forty-hour workweeks, and sick leave."

"Law societies, the certified public accountants, even engineering associations, are all examples of membership groups that help control labor supply and prevent wages from sinking. Where do you think they modeled their organization from; capitalists or unions?

"Both unions and business executives have the same problems. When people gather in tightly captive groups based on economic gain, they avoid having conversations with opposing views contrary to the majority. Their political and economic attitudes become set in stone, and they shun members who venture to speak against the prevailing popular bargaining positions."

"Union members like truck drivers or mine workers live in a separate reality than the managers who oversee the enterprise. This hardness of an 'us against them' mindset causes discerning thinking to go out the window. Whether union or management, the other side sees all conversations as critical of them."

"You sound anti-business here. So, do you believe unions are good and management bad?" Will asked, deciding to pretend Morgan was on his speakerphone.

"Of course not. I am both pro-business and pro-union. It's best if both sides get what they want. It's challenging for enterprise owners to grow to the point they can hire dozens or thousands of workers. Without expanding businesses, there would be fewer jobs. On the other hand, employees need to stick together to avoid abusive management practices."

"There is a wide variety of characters with different agendas and goals inside union organizations, and such divergent thinking causes great friction and chaos."

"Like everywhere else, you will see union head blocking membership based on racism, sexism, and xenophobia. Power struggles and jockeying for positions[lxxxvi]. Kickbacks and bribes to make deals happen. Involvement in organized crime, so gangs don't harass or steal from unions themselves."

"This is some juicy stuff. Care to elaborate?" Will wanted more.

"Moving on. Unions in private businesses are shut out of representing most workers. Less than ten percent of American employees hold union cards, and most of those are government and school workers."

"Some blame unions for striking so long and hard that some businesses have had to go bankrupt. That is not true. Circumstances beyond their control outmaneuvered alliances of workers. Globalization and automation of the factory floor have pushed out many union workers, and ironically, the union reps get significant blame for not stopping this from happening."

"The expert classes neglected to give loyalty to their brothers in blue-collar shirts and did nothing to stop the implosion of labor unions. This class divide was not surprising considering how we are socialized to separate ourselves into groups fighting over limited resources."

"Now the executives and shareholders are looking at how to trim the costs of white-collar workers as well. Everyone is vulnerable in this take no prisoners, zero-sum game of winners and losers."

Morgan paused this narration from the radio speakers and slowly materialized into the passenger seat next to Will. He looked like the genie from the magical lamp, emerging from the stereo deck.

"There, that is better. If you pull over here, I will give you some space. We can continue tomorrow, okay?"

"All right, see you tomorrow." Will allowed his passenger to exit and carried on his way.

RULE OF PRINCIPLE 23: *Avoid gossip and bragging, even if all the popular kids (& adults) are doing it. Please don't destroy people's reputation with false words. Really bad behavior!!! Do not spread false stories that may damage the reputation or business of others. (Unions and their managers did this to each other & this entrenched their positions) You do not know the facts. You do not know the consequences of your actions.*

36. Night 13 - HARASSMENT

He was making a homemade hamburger when the phone rang. "Hello?"

The caller did not respond even when Will said hello again.

For some reason, he decided to wait rather than hang up immediately. Something was different about this call.

There was no static or buzz, or ringing sound from the phone. Nothing. Not even breathing.

Will waited another ten, twenty seconds. Whatever the callers game was, he would not give him the satisfaction of yelling into the phone or losing his temper.

Will resisted the urge to say something. He was not going to lose this battle.

When the caller hung up, the disconnected line's familiar sound brought him back to the reality of his dull room and bland meal. The caller was no telemarketer, friend, or mistake. The presence on the phone was not friendly.

He picked up his hamburger and salad from the kitchen and headed into the kitchen.

37. Religion - Engage In Spirituality Daily For Inspiration & Guidance

Will and Morgan found themselves sitting in a huge Catholic church with stained glass windows. This church was one of the last remaining congregations in the city that held late-night mass every night. There were about a dozen elderly parishioners in the first three pews.

Will decided to pick the last row to share a private conversation in whispered tones without disturbing the other attendees. If anyone came near them, they would just see Will praying out loud to himself.

Morgan leaned forward on the top of the row in front of them and began:

"People get very offended when thought leaders waste criticism against any religious organization. Attacking the church is akin to attacking the Lord. I say religion is not a part of God but a pathway to him. That's why many evildoers are attracted to participating in activities within the religious community. Evil knows the safest place to hide is next to divinity."

"Are you telling me that there is a God, and he is protecting us from our dark side?" asked Will.

"I can't confirm or deny the existence of God, only that there is good and evil in each of us. Some religious folks believe that we have a guardian angel or a devil near us, influencing our behaviors. I have to dismantle that notion right now. It's you doing it. Don't blame angels or devils for your good fortune or misdeeds."

Non-believers are those who can't see any value in religion because they have had bad experiences with it. That is a mistake. Gathering in groups to commune with God has been a great boon to those without hope or meaning. Can you measure the impact of how these teachers of wisdom and humanity have on the wellbeing of billions of believers?"

"The rituals of prayer and Sunday worship have given structure and a sense of stability within chaos to those struggling to find reasons to keep moving with life. Imagine the cumulative happiness of marriages, births, parties, and friendships formed within the walls of the house of God? Such thoughts warm the heart and give hope for a greater future."

"Yet, all these benefits have come at a grand cost. The teachings of religious institutions have exacted a great toll on the psychological wellbeing of their members."

"It is challenging to extract the misdeeds and wickedness of the wrongful proprietors who have harmed their flock by plundering the teachings of the major religions, and that is why few dare to criticize spiritual organizations at all. Nevertheless, these institutions have:

1. Terrorized disciples, including children, with the belief they were in continuous danger of suffering God's wrath for the smallest sins.
2. Encouraged the poverty and discontentment of members to keep them in misery & under control of the church.
3. Allowed the destruction of nations and enslavement of peoples in the name of God's will that humans shall have dominion over all they see.
4. Accepted masculine dominance of war and aggression as supreme, which relegated feminine nurturing & caregiving to a minor role of daily religious teaching.
5. Destroyed their perceived enemies, including prosecuting Jews, Muslims, pagans, witches, and scientists, going so far as to burning victims at the stake.
6. Denied our natural roles in nature, such as having sexual desires, same-sex preferences, and other biological functions causing great confusion & anxiety.
7. Restricted access to knowledge by limiting education to the wealthier classes & banning subversive books and science experiments of the renaissance.
8. Exhorted the crusades, revolutions, and wars to start, raising their armies, causing many deaths & injuries in the process.

9. Hid the shameful betrayal of pervasive child abuse by thousands of priests throughout centuries, blocking investigations, and paying off authorities.

"Some say who cares? The transgressions of all religions are all in the past. I don't think so. We have no idea how the sins of previous generations compound and affect the behavior of humans of today."

"I am less concerned about religious folk who actively participate in prayer and community services as I am with those who have completely abandoned spiritually while still harboring the worst teachings of Christianity as they rampage through business and war."

"Imagine this. There are business leaders, bureaucrats, and politicians who believe things like 'survival of the fittest,' 'it's a dog eat dog world,' 'win at all costs', and 'if you are not with us, you are against us.' "

"Now add traditional beliefs like 'the poor are lazy,' 'non-believers should be punished by God,' 'the love of money is a sin,' and 'men must have dominion over their women, children, and slaves.' Mixing these ideas without a code of honor creates conditions where some capitalists will harm others to make meaning out of their lives."

"Having these beliefs, while ignoring the best teachings of spirituality, is part of the reason why capitalism is so brutal and unjust towards everyone who is not part of the upper stratosphere. Many people act, instruct, and

manage others with this ancient programming running silently in their minds and then wonder why conflict and disharmony teem in the world?"

"I don't know how to process that. Can I ask a completely different question that is a bit off-topic?" asked Will.

"Go ahead. All questions fit under the umbrella of spirituality."

"Why do some nutjobs believe in conspiracy theories? Millions think that lizard people disguised with human skin live among us and control a world government. Other groups think the earth is flat, and NASA faked the moon landings. At the same time, they refuse to accept concepts like good government, gender & racial equality, and world peace?" asked Will.

"Ahh, you have been thinking deep thoughts about public irrationality and voter ignorance. These conspiracy theorists have intuitive wisdom that something is wrong with the world. It's a gut feeling that is available to all humans. They also have the same feelings of stress, anxiety, and worry as everyone else but do not know where to find the answers."

"This gut anxiety & fear forces them to search for clues, but because they do not trust liberals or scientists, they need to create something tangible out of thin air to resolve these perplexing questions. Even an outlandish theory like lizard people in human suits is more logical than leaving the source of their discomfort unresolved."

"When some people live in a world where others are clearly good or bad, it is tough for their mind to comprehend that their trusted financial advisor or church leader could be ripping them off. That is why they create Zion conspiracies, Stonemason Masterminds controlling banks, Nazi henchmen living in Brazil, or aliens from outer space in their minds. Their reasoning might be a protective device to block the possibility that the world is far more complicated than their ability to process all the factors that influence their lives.

"Okay. I guess that is a misguided version of having faith in the unexplainable." Will theorized.

"Having criticized religious institutions in general, I would like to praise one community. In my opinion, they might do a better job of instilling healthy beliefs and values than almost anyone else, including most physicians, athletes, soldiers, artists, yogis, executives, and priests."

"All right, whom are you talking about?" Will asked.

"Mormons of the Christian faith."

Will was taken aback, "Are you serious?"

"Dead serious. While I completely disagree with most of the Mormon spiritual doctrine, this community has established strong foundations or pillars that both support good behavior and consideration for their fellow humans."

"As they raise children to be polite, well mannered, and disciplined hard workers, the Mormons maintain traditions of community, church, and family while completing post-secondary education and beyond. Children in tight-knit communities receive both the loving support and discipline they need because dozens of community members are there to guide them."

"Unlike members of most other religions, Mormons travel and volunteer to work for two years or longer in developing nations' cultures. Volunteering in other cultures indicates they learn to speak several languages and are tougher, wiser, more resilient to overcome challenges."

"This familiarity with poverty and lack encourages frugality and entrepreneurship. Family-run businesses create a dynamic culture where managers establish strong moral values for it to survive and thrive. Numerous studies reveal that Mormons have longer lifespans, stronger marriages, and healthier communities than most Americans."

"I guess you are saying we can learn from people even if we disagree with their culture and values?" Will guessed.

"Yes, remember, since every person and group has pieces of lightness and darkness in them, you can emulate their higher qualities and ignore their failings to assemble the best life choices that you can make."

"That makes sense. Thank you for that," Will said.

RULE OF PRINCIPLE 24: *The odds are you are a morally kind person regardless of your spiritual affinity. Disbelieving in God or organized religion does not make you a sinful person & hiding inside one does not excuse wickedness. Your actions and deeds create your good character, not your association with a spiritual group.*

Participating in spiritual rituals is a wise practice because being morally upright is more a daily practice than a state of mind. We require weekly reminders to consider our communities' holy needs but don't feel guilty if a busy life prevents you from attending worship.

38. Internet Spying - Do Not Computer Hack, Steal files or Troll Strangers

Eight young boys in traditional Christian robes emerged from a side door near the pulpit and assembled at the pews' front. This choir was there to practice hymns for the next Sunday mass. As they practiced musical scales, Will and Morgan lost interest in the background melodies and resumed their conversation.

"Do you want to know the reason that the world is turning away from ethics and morality? We are in a 'free for all' economy where no one culture sets all the rules or controls participants' behavior. Of course, what keeps capitalism spinning out of control is many traditional customs and morals from Christianity baked into trade agreements and international rules of law."

"But this newly networked society only protects those in power, and other countries can spy and attack their neighbors online without punishment or censure. Borders and laws are of no concern. Foreign agencies regularly are spying and attacking citizens of other countries with little threat of punishment or censure."

"It's challenging to measure how pervasive the threat of online theft, spying, and terrorism. We still have this image of teenage hackers working alone in dirty & dark rooms, brilliantly breaking into banks and govt computer networks, but that is a fraction of the problem."

"Picture tens of thousands of people in thousands of rooms around the world, monitoring and watching internet users as they go online shopping or chat in underground forums and public spaces like Facebook and Twitter. Countless government agencies & secretrative businesses employ these 'Peeping Toms' to maintain order and control over their populace."

"Independent program hackers and government organizations can steal data, information, and even digital currency for their own end goals. This data can be sold on the black market by private citizens or traded to gain power and influence with autocratic leaders and gang bosses."

"Many computer programmers create email viruses, online robots or software designed to anger, confuse and disrupt political elections or peaceful protests. By slowing down and breaking up movements, governments can block threats to their power before they happen."

"Hackers can impersonate members of a political party and write vicious and mean statements online to rile up the opposing party members. When the political parties of rival nations can't agree on policies, it can be a competitive advantage for corrupt countries and corporations when negotiating foreign trade or environmental treaties."

"Modern technology that allows users to sabotage strangers tens of thousands of miles away is devious because designing programs that travel over a long distance does not feel like a brutal, violent act to the predator. "

"The victim has been dehumanized because they are only images and words on a screen. The hacker is praised and encouraged with work and money, so they continue this work without regard to the consequences. The weapons themselves are nothing but coding, programs, and software that has little to distinguish itself from normal programming."

"In short, we have removed the emotions and humanity from an evil act, and that helps the participants rationally detach themselves from wrongdoing without too little negative distress, guilt, or shame."

"Local police often ignore this underground criminal behavior because authorities have little sympathy for wealthy white foreigners who do not care to know anything about their emerging country. The police in less developed countries are solving crimes in their jurisdiction and do not have the resources to participate in fighting international corruption."

"What people don't realize is the vast majority of business transactions are in the process of becoming digitalized, and if ninety-nine percent of currency is electronic, then that is where governments, spy networks, and criminal gangs will spend their time. They will be on the internet, trading drugs, humans, weapons, gold, diamonds, and banned goods, wrecking lives, and stealing futures."

"This is one of the greatest challenges of future economies. Tens of millions of programmers will be instigating invasive incursions among billions of internet users to steal wealth and data for those who pay for it. Uncountless numbers experience violation without ever seeing the face of their attackers."

"Aren't most hackers young people under the age of thirty?" Will asked.

"Many young people feel lost and isolated, especially if they do not have healthy social skills. Participating in hacking and spying allows them to gain a sense of purpose, a venue to challenge themselves and others, and a place to belong."

"Imagine how you were in your teens, eager to drink, smoke, and do stupid things so other kids would think you were cool. Computer hacking is nothing compared to other riskier behaviors that teens try to fit in."

"Families must establish rules and disciplines of how to conduct themselves on the internet; otherwise, the ramifications could be horrific. I am unaware of any movement to teach modern morality and ethics in a global & digitally connected world, so protections will continue to deteriorate. Right now, consumers use the internet like they use television - mindlessly. "

"Without a moral compass, we will again fall prey to the worst impulses of our dark side. Greed, envy, anger, depression, jealousy, lust, and aggression will reign over people as they fight to earn money and gain status on platforms filled with millions of strangers."

"I am so sorry to be this bleak, but my purpose is to teach & illuminate the truth. Not distract you with fairy tales. Today we are focusing on the nasty side of the internet to prepare us for the worst yet to come."

Will and Morgan got up and left the church. What energy Will had disappeared, and suddenly he felt weary. Instead of stopping to rest, he asked Morgan to help him get home. "C'mon, I got ya." Morgan let Will drape his arm over his neck. The engineer found himself staring at his doorstep. He had no idea how he got back.

RULE OF PRINCIPLE 25 - *Do not hack into computers, steal files or troll strangers. Just because you can't recognize your victims' faces or live in another country, it does not make internet vandalism acceptable. Immoral behavior online is just as bad as in person.*

Adults have failed to teach ethical conduct online as a community effort, and all children suffer in one way or another from this negligence. Parents need to understand when to punish their children and when to be their friend. If parents neglect their duties, merchants, criminals, and other children will teach inauthentic morality and ethics instead.

39. Night 14 - KINKY

Angel wrecked his plans. He had picked her up to treat her to a fancy French restaurant. The couple was driving to their destination when she upended the game plan. When the blonde saw a cute little independent hotel on the side of the road, she demanded Will pull over. Angel just had to scratch that itch now, and he was not going to dispute such a fantastic idea.

The desk clerk raised his eyebrow. A bit giddy with joy, the handsome couple, arriving with no luggage or bags, had asked for one night with no reservations. Being discrete, he said nothing but snuck a knowing smile at the pair as the elevator doors concealed their romantic embrace.

She loved being picked up and twirled around like a kid, so he lifted her off her feet as the elevator doors opened. Will carried her to the suite door. 'Your room, madam,' he proclaimed as if he was a butler serving his lady. The giggling noise subsided as they closed the door.

40. Government Agencies - Protest Domestic Spying & Stealing Of Further Liberties

A German sedan roared down the highway at untenable speeds well above the legal speed limit. No police cruiser would have let this vehicle pass without turning on its sirens. Fortunately for Will, there was no law and order presence along this stretch of road.

Morgan revealed himself to be a speed demon. While they raced through these concrete ribbons, he began speaking as if it was nothing, as if they were strolling through the park.

"Where wars end, the forces that cause all this physical violence and destruction do not disappear, anger and fear transform and are driven underground, behind closed doors."

"What are you talking about?" Will asked.

"The counterintelligence sector. Since the last world war, military organizations have withdrawn from the field of battle and have transformed into bureaucracies, watching & waiting for new dangers. Spying on foreign rivals and domestic citizens is now a dynamic government industry with tentacles in every nation and every island.

Will was bored, "Like the James Bond films? I don't see how this can involve the dark side of humankind?"

"Come on now! Can't you see it? The shadow is very suspicious of others. It can only see the worst in others. Agents watch each other, collect information, trade secrets, and double-cross their counterparts with false information[lxxxvii]. All in the hope of uncovering national security files that expose a weakness their country can exploit."

"Our agents are on guard, waiting for attacks, rather than taking steps to embrace common rivals to solve problems together like climate change, nuclear weapons, and global poverty. Unlike chess and other games, spying never ends, and there are no winners."

"Every country, whether democratic or authoritarian, spies on its people with deeper concentration than they do on foreign agents. Spying is necessary because the local police can't investigate subversive activities outside the criminal code."

"Ordinary people commit a wide variety of crimes before they get their first conviction or are aiding terrorists or criminal gangs from other countries. Government monitoring is essential for protecting society when police organizations have no jurisdiction."

Will guessed, "So spying helps to prevent crime and terrorism."

"True, and yet this benefit is widely exaggerated and propagandized to keep taxpayers from discovering the real truth."

"What truth?" Will asked.

"When elites accumulate wealth, and the aristocracies are separated from the rest of the population by deep systemic economic unfairness, the wealthy invest in more security, more armies, more prisons, more police, and more spies."

"Spy agencies in all countries have proliferated especially since 2001, and it's not to protect the average citizen. They are spying on everyone around the world to protect the elites from disruptive forces to the accumulation of wealth."

"That sounds like paranoia. I did not know you were a conspiracy theorist," he commented.

"When every country is spying on its citizens, conspiracy is a poor choice of word. It's not that great a leap of imagination. Multinational corporations are shipping goods worldwide on international waters and have enormous sums of money and data circling the globe. These businesses pressure their governments to spy on everyone to prevent the theft of data, patents, money, and goods by international gangs, hostile governments, or even employees. Governments capitulate from financial pressures and request their agencies to investigate malicious parties."

Morgan throttled down to a lower gear, and the BMW sped along at the legal limit.

"The secrecy of these spy organizations allows the increased bureaucracy and abuse that falls down this waste hole of taxpayer dollars. We have no idea whether agencies spend funds wisely and how many crimes or acts of terrorism are arrested."

Will expanded this theory, "So you mean spies are listening to telephone conversations, searching on computer networks, watching people on cameras and following them in person so that enterprises can keep moving along?"

"And within this community, abuses also happen. Globally, hundreds of thousands of people work in spy agencies. With such power to investigate and arrest anarchists, socialists, and protestors, some agents have let their dark side get the best of them."

"There has been a history of injustice in every country when senior directors at government agencies had used their powers to harass, destroy or even injury & kill their enemies when legally they had no right to do so."

"The federal police have almost unlimited power, and the courts often grant them search warrants and subpoenas based on hearsay - suspicious conversations and wispy gossip. Whether successful or not, agents have damaged and taken the property of innocent civilians who had no criminal history or reason to be investigated."

"You remember the FBI and IRS harassing black celebrities and activists during the civil rights movement? Homeland agents arrested many innocent Muslims shortly after 2001? How about federal officers who tried to hurt the careers of supposedly communist sympathizers during the fifties? Can you see violations of their civil rights are forerunners of the breach of your rights?"

"I had no idea. I thought this stuff only happened in Soviet Russia or right now in Communist China," Will replied.

"Spying is everywhere. It never ceases. As long as humans continue to feel fear and anxiety about the future, they will seek damning information to alleviate that worry. No matter how much blood, sweat, and tears, the shadow will seek to watch and destroy all that challenges what is familiar and safe."

"And do you know why this conflict never ends?"

"No. I don't," Will admitted softly.

"Because we deny the existence of death. We don't see the common humanity in our foes and forget they also want to stop all wars, to live in peace. All of our enemies also have birthdays, illnesses, and family problems. Humans don't recognize that we are all spirits traveling the same path. Instead, we are undisciplined materialists plagued with the superficiality and boredom of modern life."

"By representing that we won't die, we disconnect from religion, community, and purpose.[lxxxviii] Then caught between the brutal cruelty of our work, and the empty pleasures of drinking, partying, and television, we turn on one another."

"This society seeks the growth of technology, systems, energy sources at the expense of human potential and wellness. When we construct a safe and sanitized world from our natural place in the food chain, we forget we need each other to survive. This break from the natural order of things causes us to invent stories of imagined conflicts, aggression, and threats. Spying has become the natural progression of humanity for all these reasons."

The off-ramp was ahead. The men spied a brilliantly lit gas station-restaurant that was a popular resting stop for drivers and truckers alike. Morgan exited the roadway and parked the car, and said: "You take over. Are we going anywhere in particular?"

"Nah, let's go home." Will decided.

RULE OF PRINCIPLE 26: *Accept the world as is and it is yours. Be tolerant and accepting of religious and political views that are different from yours. Do not try to hurt people because you don't like their ideas, personalities, appearance, or tastes.*

Separate the opinions and beliefs from the person expressing them and realize this is a human being just like you. Criticize lousy behavior and not people's good name. When you try to censor others, the powerful will gain strength to regulate everyone they don't like, including you.

41. Outsourced Manufacturing -Think Globally, Act Locally Is Not A Slogan

Now that Will was back in the driver's seat, he could breathe again. Not that he did not trust Morgan. It was just that the young man felt unsettled, letting his imagination propel the vehicle forward. He turned the car around and took the highway back into the city.

"Human beings are so adverse to the complex and unfamiliar that they would rather work extremely hard in an inefficient and unethical traditional manufacturing market than reform the system and reap the benefits."

"I don't understand. Yes, people are resistant to change, but what needs fixing in manufacturing?" Will asked.

"Unsurprisingly, some people will fight for and defend the rights of their fellow citizens but completely ignore the same worker rights in other countries. They can't see we are living in a global economy where practices in one region with different cultures can spread to their domain."

"Oh, you are talking about the offshoring of manufacturing jobs to poorer countries. How can we stop that? Corporations can do anything they want." Will declared.

"That thinking is a product of your impoverished educational system that demands compliance and obedience over morals, principles, and negotiated agreements."

"Consumers can do something by voting with their wallets to purchase goods made only in safe and fair working conditions. But that is not enough. We are talking about reforming a morally bankrupt system that ruins workers in the Americas, Europe, Africa and Asia, alike."

"Many people will defend this economic system, even if it is crushing them, simply out of national pride and social cohesion. Their place in the corporate hierarchy, as well as perceived friendships, are in jeopardy if they complain against unfairness and criminality in the workplace.[lxxxix]"

"Oh, I get it. The 'keep your mouth shut' rule. How do employee ethics come into play with global manufacturing? Will was full of questions.

"Schooling is not just to learn English, Math, and Science. Students receive education to become familiar and dependent on the status quo with its inequalities and power abuses. We learn to become afraid of authority, and this is why many will not speak out against police brutality, employer abuse, and corrupt dictatorships."

"Corporations doubled down by introducing cultures of positive psychology & public relations. To keep our livelihoods, we must always act positive and speak well of our companies and their products in public."

"Negativity and complaining are discouraged. Critics of the system are transferred, demoted, fired, or shunned. Nobody wants to defend the workers of countries they don't live in if it means the loss of employment or advancement."

"But even these poor working conditions are helping countries develop and build up their wealth. Maybe someday they can become rich too?" Will countered.

"Not so. Technology and global competition are moving too fast to predict the future. Still, it's unlikely that manufacturing in poorer countries will produce the kind of middle class that Europe and America created in the last century."

"We are so ignorant about what is happening in the world because diversions are stealing away our attention from dangers. Many wealthy consumers believe that factory jobs in Asia and Africa are dehumanizing but are much better than not having any jobs. "

"Workers from farmlands are forced or have incentives to move into industrialized jobs but get trapped in a new cycle of survival & poverty. Ten to fourteen-hour days working on an assembly line or a sewing machine, getting paid one to three dollars per hour is a troublesome life. It is without question that workers can't build a prosperous life on that income."

"The supervisors pressure the employees to keep up the pace and threaten slower workers with layoffs. Many factories do not provide adequate dining rooms, washrooms, fire escapes, or protective gear, so the workers are at risk of injury or illness."

Will swerved left to avoid a piece of debris on the road. The two occupants flopped to their left sides before gaining equilibrium.

"Business managers justify unsafe working conditions and low wages by saying the competition is so fierce that they must cut costs. If they don't underpay workers, they will have to close shop, and then some other factory owner will exploit the laborers. And they are right."

"It's the fashion, furniture, food or technology companies in wealthier countries that put their brands on the products which compensate developing nation factories. They, as the customer, are ultimately responsible for horrible working conditions. "

"Some executives in a shiny glass office decided to cut costs and shift production from clean, regulated, and safe factories to hidden places. Dirty, hot, and poorly monitored factories that don't have high tax and environmental charges to bear."

"The powerless workers of these emerging countries take on this price. Low wages imply stunted tax revenue for schools, hospitals, and community centers. Lax regulation means factories can dump waste into waterways and near homes. We are destroying lives and the planet all in the name of cheap products and large profit margins."

"Some people say so what! It's not their problem. I say wrong! Human misery spreads and contaminates lands far away. Pollution travels globally. Criminality crosses borders. Financial inequality is getting worse in every country. Migrants are on the march for better jobs. Job standards & regulations are under pressure everywhere. It is a global problem."

Will gave his opinion, "I agree. It's just going to be hard to get people to change their spending habits."

"People can't see that there are countless ways to redesign and revolutionize our supply and demand chains. When our attitudes change, kindness will follow."

 What a rude spirit, Will thought, as he pulled onto his street. Morgan disappeared again without the common courtesy of saying goodbye. But should that be his primary concern at the moment? The manners of a person who existed only in his mind? Could he reasonably call himself mentally balanced if he was spending time with his hallucinations? He wondered when this adventure was going to end.

RULE OF PRINCIPLE 27: *Please don't beat yourself up for feeling confused because it's complicated to understand the rules of life as each culture has its own. It requires twenty years to become an adult and another twenty to realize that half of what you believe to be true is held together by lies and duct tape.*

Multinational corporations are counting on xenophobia, nationalism, and ignorance to divide global workforces and natural resources to exploit the earth's wealth. Wealthier consumers would benefit financially by helping developing nations' workers rise up and demand higher pay and safer working conditions.

42. Night 15 -THRILLING

Getting another text from Angel was like scratching out a winning lotto ticket and getting to play again. Will was thrilled to see that they were developing that fun back and forth pattern that got their original relationship off to a bang.

He suggested using video chat on their mobile devices and pressed the button when she rang him up. Angel's glowing, perfect features filled up his screen, and he got that same emotional charge that he always did whenever a beautiful woman crossed his path.

She teased him about the T-shirt he was wearing, and he complimented her on the necklace around her neck. Then she gently reminded Will that he had bought it for her as a Christmas gift. He remembered. Civil engineers could have good taste on occasion.

Will asked her about her parents and sisters. Why do you want to know about my family? Why so many questions? she asked. He replied that he was insatiable in his appetite to know her. When he could see their stories in her eyes, he would experience her in a way nobody else can.

Will had a growing pit of nervousness in his stomach between the lapses in conversation that something about this conversation was not entirely natural. Why now? Why did she come back to him?

He knew he had gained a bit of weiht and looked haggard from a lack of sleep. Angel was too charming to mention that she could see he lacked the physical strength and vitality from two years ago. He decided to keep playing this game to see what happened next.

43. Vulture Capitalists - Don't Invest In Wicked Business Practices

Will was so tired that he thought the shadows on his bedroom walls were moving and dancing. It was four AM in the morning, and the only light was coming from the nightlight plugged in near the bottom of the closet door.

As he lay in bed, he thought about how uncomfortable his life had become in the last three weeks. This rumination mixed all the mistakes in his life with all the worst things he had learned about humanity's transgressions. Will felt depressed, worried, and exhausted.

"Morgan, why are you torturing me with this stuff? I just want to be left alone." Will cried out into the empty room.

"Will, you jerk, I told you dozens of times you are doing this to yourself. I am a manifestation of your subconscious trying to talk to you to get you straight" Morgan opened the bedroom door and appeared as a hazy shadow in the door frame.

"Okay, fine. I would rather sleep than learn what a sh*tshow this planet has become," the young man remarked.

"Very soon it will be over. We are downloading much data into your brain as Morpheus did to Neo in 'The Matrix.' Remember that martial arts scene?"

"Yeah, I do. I guess I might as well learn something," Will agreed.

"Do you think capitalism is a completely evil way to employ workers and turn resources into goods and services?" Morgan asked.

"Of course not. It's the best system we have got," said Will.

"Yes, it is a tool just like an ax or hammer. Commerce can be used to build things or destroy the past. It's all in the intent of whether capitalism hurts or harms others."

"When managers and executives of capitalistic organizations deny their shadow side and all the flaws within, they tend to rage against obstacles and lose their compassion for those who are less fortunate.[xc] "

"So does capitalism make participants rotten, or do cruel people enjoy using capitalism to run over others?" asked Will

"That is an excellent 'chicken and egg' question. Yes, and yes. An essential feature of capitalism is for more energetic companies to force weaker companies out of business by giving better services or prices. That way, bad actors are punished for not doing the work demanded by the market, and customers benefit by getting more value for their money."

"Some capitalists don't want to play fair by offering superior services or goods. They grow by manipulating and controlling their competitors and the industry. Some companies realize it's faster to acquire and merge with other companies than to grow naturally [xci]."

"They grow by living off the misery of struggling companies that need help or by forcing healthy companies into bankruptcy. Most of the public are not aware that many companies who could provide employment are purchased and broken up, sold for parts."

"These predators take advantage of the blame culture, which points fingers everywhere and demands that someone else is at fault for failing business practices. The vulture capitalists swoop in while the existing managers are infighting and purchase controlling shares before they are fought off."

"So the vulture capitalists take advantage of our weakness because we don't take responsibility to fix problems?" asked Will.

"Yes. When businesses get into financial trouble and need loans or cash investments, it is often the employees who suffer. For example, **during mergers and acquisitions, employees can lose tens of thousands of dollars in lost pay because managers eliminate redundant positions and layoff workers to trim the fat. 'The losers' are awarded long periods of unemployment or early retirement, and larger & more stressful workloads are**

given to the 'winners.' All to squeeze more profits out of otherwise viable businesses."

"Okay, you mentioned before that mergers and layoffs trigger our dark sides so that we become more anxious, fearful, worried, depressed, and angry," said Will.

"It's dreadful for everyone, including the affluent, when moneyed companies buy out weaker firms to fire employees and influence market forces. When there are fewer competitors, prices increase, selection decreases, and service quality declines."

"It's normal for healthy businesses to fall into trouble due to downturns in the economy and changes in technology. Instead of fixing or modernizing these dependable firms for much broader long term profits over many years, the vulture capitalists go for quick cash and close out the business."

"So what? People find jobs elsewhere, right?" Will asked.

"Not always. Sometimes this disruption to employment leads to suicide, chronic unemployment, and the death of towns. People can be very resilient and tough, but if you create an economy where businesses are buying and selling assets of other companies instead of producing real goods and services, you will destabilize a precarious workforce."

"Imagine a world where companies find it more profitable to hire and fire people seasonally than keep them for the long term. When businesses engage in massive risk-taking and borrowing, the economy matures into a roller coaster of recessions and expansions. Picture many businesses going bankrupt because they took on too much debt to fight off acquisitions or expand through mergers. Such greed looks attractive today but is foolish behavior in the end!"

"Observe how such an economy could stress out workers and cause worries whether they would have a job tomorrow. Imagine a country where it's normal for employees to become unemployed for months every couple of years throughout their working life. I can project many with insecure employment will give up dreams of college, children, marriage, and buying homes."

"Now, I get it! When capitalists become vultures, they engage in evil and wicked practices that can cause many employees financial and psychological distress due to layoffs, shortened hours, and slashed bonuses," said Will.

"Yes, you are very right about the psychical stress of a poorly regulated, out of control economy that allows businesses to be bought, sold and dismantled like sports trading cards."

"One author wrote many years ago that most children in the kindergarten classes he attended behave better than the adults around them. These children share everything, pledge not to harm their classmates, clean up after themselves, put things back as they found them, apologize for hurting others, hold hands and stick together, and don't take things that don't belong to them.[xcii] Many capitalists could learn a thing or two from these children."

RULE OF PRINCIPLE 28: *Please teach your children to be polite. Ethical citizens tend to display polite manners as a sign of intelligence and mutual respect. As people assert their individuality and feel free to behave as they see fit, good manners become even more important to show respect for others.*

Please be polite, say thank you, hold doors open and don't shove or touch. Agreeable manners help open discussions so opposing forces can gather together to solve difficulties. Thank you for allowing me to share this with you.

44. Worker Compensation - Vast Executive & Celebrity Pay Is Not Normal

Morgan was still standing in the doorframe and decided to come into the room and sit on Will's bed. Will was leaning on his side, so he sat up straighter, bum on the pillow, and back against the bed headboard.

"Can I ask you something? How do you know all this stuff if you are part of my subconscious? I never learned a fraction of this stuff." asked Will.

"Boy, you and every person alive doesn't know a millionth of the data in their brains. There are tens of thousands of pages of news articles, books, webpages, stories, and other information all swirling in your head. The whole history of humanity. All I am doing is taking what you know as bits and pieces and connecting the dots so you can see a bigger slice of the entire picture."

Will was speechless, so Morgan continued with the lesson.

"People do what works, even if it's screwed up behavior that hurts others. I am going to repeat this over and over until you get it."

"I got it. Okay, we will do whatever we can get away with," said Will

"For example, the need for certainty and stability within a fragile status hierarchy like the executive suite causes leaders to overpay themselves. The desire to' keep up with the Jones' is greater than the logical imperative to reinvest profits into strengthening their communities." said Morgan

"You mean CEOs are so busy measuring their paycheck against others that they neglect the well being of their employees? I don't know why workers are not bothered by that." Will remarked.

"Most don't know how to react because the subordinate workers are struggling with mental conflicts, like bills, errands, and relationships, in their heads. Employees deny these problems and rob themselves of the opportunity to solve them. Instead of admitting that there is a structural compensation problem within organizations, some blame themselves for low pay by thinking they are not working hard enough."

"Some switch to other corporations in a vain attempt to climb the career ladder. Few will burst out of the toxic positivity culture that prevents decent and rancor. Complaining about your managers' boss and his unethical choices is career suicide."

"Employees don't know whether the financial situation of their companies is healthy or poor, so managers feel free to overpay star salespeople and programmers who have jobs that can make a big difference to the bottom line. Many executives and their board members have slashed research departments or trimmed the quality of the products or services to squeeze more money out of their business."

Will described his workplace: "I knew something was up in my company, but I could not put my finger on it. We don't discuss salaries, and we don't question strategy at my job. We just work the job and let the managers make the decisions. That's a fair compromise, is it not?"

"It would be if salaries were open and transparent. People might not be gossiping, infighting, and undermining their colleagues if bosses distribute compensation uniformly based on skill, seniority, and other factors. "

"Employees deny their negative emotions with false positivity to keep the appearance of workplace happiness, which creates additional dysfunction and chronic rage and anxiety throughout their career."

"When inexperienced, agreeable workers do not set boundaries for pay and treatment, more aggressive and dominant managers weld their power unfairly. We let co-workers hurt us and then feel regret for not standing up for what is right."

"If you wonder why you feel exhausted, even in an office setting, here is one cause. Our dark sides are in conflict with our light sides and a battle with everyone else's dark side. Each of us uses up our power, willpower, social power, and generosity power every day.[xciii] That makes us emotionally infirm by the end of the day, and then we rise with the sun, refreshed, to begin new battles again."

"Executives are earning billions while their workers struggle-that is the public story that is spinning to be acceptable to the masses. Not many know the whole story."

"Corporations do all sorts of unethical tricks behind closed doors and maneuvering to suck revenue into private pockets. We are talking about embezzlement in the billions, black market transactions, kickbacks, trading inflated deals to pad the bottom line. "

"There are thousands of government investigators in the FBI and IRS and other European agencies trying to trace and locate some of this money. Companies are sheltering income in tax havens and offshoring tasks to poor Asian and Latin American countries. All this while fighting revenue collectors in court, receiving sales & property tax breaks from cities & states as well as denying workers inflationary wage increases."

"And they are getting away with this. I hear nothing about this in the news. Politicians, news media, church leaders, and academics are bought and paid for by corporate leadership. They all trade favors keeping this scam going." Will carried on.

"That's good. Very good that you know this. Impressive," said Morgan. So can you guess how this manifests into an eruption of the dark side?

"Well, based on my own life, I felt frustration and fear when my bosses denied promotions and a raise in pay, which created a wave of deep anger that I let out at car drivers. And then on terrible days, my ex-wife and I would tear into one another, each blaming the other for overspending and past due bills," Will replied.

"Yes, you see how participating in the corporate environment fuels anger, fear, resentment, depression, and every other dark emotion for millions of people? Marriages splatter, relationships shatter, and friends scatter all because we can't keep our emotions in check long enough to see the problem at hand?"

Morgan got off the bed and walked to Will's closet. He opened the door and looked inside. "Nice threads" as if the revelation did not know everything about Will already. He turned around and peered from behind the door mischievously. Morgan's eyes twinkled as he turned around again and walked into the closet shutting the door behind him.

Will leaped out of his bed like a trampoline jumper and rushed to the closet. Nope. Morgan was not hiding inside. He had left. Will signed, scratched the itchy parts of his torso, and climbed back under the sheets.

RULE OF PRINCIPLE 29 - *Lying is not harmless. Please try to be more honest by picking and choosing the right times to lie. If the average person lies between 60,000 and 120,000 times in their lifetime, blunt honesty will make you an unwelcome outcast. So the question is not whether to lie or not, but how often and when? Maybe, we could cut down our lying by ten to twenty-five percent? Perhaps be a little more discrete in the use of deception?*

45. Night 16 - DIFFERENCES

Sitting on his sofa, watching some antique pawn reality show, Will found his mind drifting back to his girlfriend. Ex-girlfriend? A friend with benefits? He was not sure what he could label this current version of their relationship.

He desperately wanted to chat with her. Impulsively he began typing her a question. Where is this relationship going? Then his instincts kicked in. No, that would be a mistake. Will erased his words and asked a new question: Do opposites like us attract? Are we an exception to the rule?

Angel seemed to have a knack for analyzing relationships to their core. She found these types of questions irresistible and replied quickly to his text. He once joked the blonde should take on an advice column like Ann Landers. She did not find that funny, saying maybe she would take his advice and become a couples counselor when the time was right.

Angel replied that she thought they were more alike than similar. Sure, she was artistic and friendly while he was studious and intellectual. She was a blonde, bubbly, and thin girl who favored bright clothes and lots of jewelry. He was dark, stocky, severe, and muscular, whose possessions included dark suits and tech gear.

They discussed their differences. Angel lit up a room by just walking in and could spend long evenings conversing with every stranger in the bar. He could slip into a place without anyone noticing and preferred to have a deep, meaningful conversation with one attractive friend for hours.

Why did they get together in the first place? Will's handsome features had caught Angels' eye. When they discovered a mutual fascination with spicy food, British films, and Latin dancing, they found they also shared traditional values about marriage, religion, children, and work. He was surprised how genuine their relationship was when she listed it all out.

Beauty and insight. She had both in abundance; Will complimented her acumens by text. Why does everyone think I am another dumb blonde? Angel complained. Not me. I knew from the start; you would enchant me in a way that would reveal myself, Will replied.

46. Low Wage Exploitation - Mature Into Positive Activism

This fast food service restaurant was one of those all-night places that recently established a new ten pm closing time. It was almost nine-thirty in the evening, and the crew was hurrying around, scrubbing the tables and floor clean, to close down for the night.

The staff was too busy to notice that the young man was sitting by himself in the corner, burger, fries, and soda untouched, talking to himself. A young couple coming off a date noticed and moved away from Will to another booth at the far corner. Another crazy homeless person, they guessed.

Will no longer cared about what people were thinking. The exhaustion and blurriness from a lack of sleep diverted power from his brain's social awareness to his rational & logical mind. He was becoming more and more fascinated with morality and evil as the nights wore on.

Morgan wanted to talk about the employer-worker dynamic. **"The dark side of people is also a curious beast. It wants to see how far it can exert its power and domination over objects and people. Some get off manipulating victims into unpaid slavery. Others can see the fear in our eyes and offer almost criminally low wages."**

"The public recognizes that some employers will exploit the most vulnerable workers who are desperate to accept very little in pay.

"People say bosses exploit workers but, collectively, our shadows let us abuse ourselves.[xciv] Some have foolish values that interpret the meaning of events to their detriment. They chose poorly and picked the least unobjectionable option in a rush to secure some income."

"What! That's pretty harsh. The world is a cruel and hostile workplace. We have to do what we can to survive." said Will

"Did your parents teach you that, or was it the media that injected that weak idea into your head? Fine, so you need money to survive, and entry-level employment is the first step out of absolute poverty and into the workforce."

Then what? Why do some take responsibility for their lives and search for something just a little better while others stay stuck in dead-end jobs and stew in front of the TV?" asked Morgan.

"I guess some workers see low wage jobs as a stepping stone. They interpret having any job as being meaningful and a great learning experience that allows them to try again for a higher-skilled position," said Will. "Pessimistic workers realize they can survive with a minimum wage and believe their situation to be a permanent dead end."

"Ahh, that's it. The workers who have an expansive, curious, and optimistic mindset don't see the minimum wage as an end but as a beginning. Too bad our economic marketplace does not reflect those ideals. Some employees get lost because commerce sticks them into places they can't escape."

"In the golden days, young students in college, immigrants, and spouses raising children could enter the workforce with few skills and be trained on the job. After gaining experience, they could work their way up to real careers."

"While this may have been true thirty or fifty years ago, tens of millions of workers are stuck at minimum wage jobs because the world economy has automatized and eliminated numerous intermediate jobs."

"My classmates and I were able to escape the minimum wage trap and..." countered Will

Morgan interrupted Will abruptly, "Because you and your classmates already had the identity and values of the professional classes, you moved to change for the better. Your sense of optimism made you ask for and receive support to complete the college-level skills required for advancement."

"Some workers have solid values of self-worth and will not accept wages that are dismissive of their talents. This conversation is not happening in the head of the typical minimum wage worker."

"What is the quality of thinking that keeps them playing small?" asked Will.

"Their dark side is full of shadowy thoughts that they are not good enough, not smart enough, not confident enough. And if their physical appearance is not what is desirable in the workplace, society's dark side is eager to spread poison in their ear."

"Marginalized workers with weight problems, disabilities, wrinkles, bad skin, or thick accents can end in this workplace. They are judged in under three seconds as not belonging in the executive offices but on the periphery. The ones who fight their way out; they don't accept the assessment that low skilled work is where they belong."

"Changing jobs requires an enormously difficult change in identity. People must state out loud, "No, I disagree with your poor judgment of me built on ancient and outdated prejudices. I demand a seat at the table. I want a job that matches my skills and abilities."

Inspired, Will said, "You have gone all Nelson Mandella on me right there. Amen Brother. Why doesn't the government do more about it?"

"Businesses influence the government to focus on job creation, not job quality. Politicians know money and voting power comes from the elites and professional classes, so it's rarely on the agenda."

"Vulnerable workers feel betrayed by the system, so they don't vote in numbers to counteract the lobbying industry that is jostling to keep wages low. Poor political representation is simply a self-fulfilling prophecy that keeps the gears of commerce spinning as they have."

"One last thing. Workers, big and small, are making choices every day. They find it disorienting and scary to make a big identity shift. Giving up low wages means giving up some of your old values of scarcity and lack. It symbolizes giving up feeling secure in your old, inane job for the feeling of being a fraud and loser in your new and sparkling job."

The dark side will fight back if you bring more light into your life. It will deceive you. Make you feel alone. Question your values. It will even make you want to die instead of stepping into the shoes of the man or woman you desire to be[xcv]. Don't ever forget that."

"Why do you have to wreck this positive vibe we just had, man? You say you want to help me, but then you make me feel awful and weak?" Will asked.

"I have my reasons…"

RULE OF PRINCIPLE 30: *Life is unfair and unjust. On the other hand, society has the right to limit power on those who abuse it. Either participate in efforts to make it fairer or let it go. Complaining about it won't help. Action will. Many awful things have happened because the silent majority said nothing and did not act. If it is safe to do so, act like how you would like your leaders to work, and inspire others to do the same.*

47. Retirement - Invest Conservatively To Build Financial Strength

A very elderly couple walked in to get some ice cream cones. Will starred in surprise, his burger half-eaten in his hands. Most seniors were in bed this late at night, and ice cream was an unusual choice in the middle of winter.

Morgan was also looking at this couple, and this inspired him to change the topic again. "The problem with you humans is that you evolved to be short-sighted. You rarely think ahead more than a week. If forced to make plans for the future, you make decisions hastily because we can only see obstacles right in front of us and none of the abundant opportunities in the distance."

"Talking about the future, the retirement and pension industry is another example of how many steal expectations away from the elderly after decades of hard work and sacrifice."

"Is it another industry full of sharks?" demanded Will.

"Both brokers and clients lie to each other that they know what they are doing. The financial industry has quietly created the perception that they run firms full of brilliant mathematical geniuses who use computers and other voodoo to create wealth out of nothing from stock and bond investing. Investors don't want to know their understanding of finance resembles those waiting for a magical goose to lay golden eggs. Stock & bond trading is often pure fantasy & wishful thinking."

"The dirty secret of Wall Street, or whatever name the money biz calls itself, is that fees, commissions, and administration costs charged to the clients generate higher profits than stock picks. Those two and a half percent mutual fund or stock trading fees generate billions of dollars. But it's never enough for some executives and salespeople."

"'Buy and hold' clients are not profitable for firms, so investment firms encourage vulnerable investors to jump from one bad investment to another. In most trades like this, the client loses a little, and the broker makes a commission. The losses do add up."

"Financial brokers, bankers, and other experts rely on inexperienced and foolish investors executing frequent purchases of stocks, bonds, commodities, and other tradable securities. Unaware savers receive insufficient information and mediocre investments based on educated guesses and fashion trends rather than sound research. Many clients don't realize how much they gave up to their investment company until retirement. Questions?"

"So people lose a little bit of money here and there. So what? Is this really about being dishonest or about being jealous of good business practices?"

"Oh, so you want to be a little capitalist bastard yourself, huh! We are talking about trillions of dollars transferred from average savers into the coffers of the rich. We are chatting about wrecking retirement plans and sending families into budget mobile homes instead of the desirable condo resorts near the beach. All under their noses. Legal, yes, morally wrong, yes."

"I don't know whom to trust anymore," said Will.

"Not everyone is dishonest. The leadership in each industry sets the standard, and the employees just follow orders to keep their jobs. Do you want to protect yourself? Educate yourself, learn the finer details of the stock market or real estate investing, and learn to trust your instincts. Find people you can trust and ask for help."

"Deception and theft work in financial markets because our shadow encourages us to feel guilt or shame for not understanding what is going on. We lack the courage to ask for help or request our agents to explain the details to our full comprehension. There is this deep feeling of isolation when making choices, and our dark side projects potential embarrassment into our minds if we were to reveal losses to others."

"The shadows of others look on in smug superiority and consolation if we complain that we were deceived or cheated on the market. Winners of this system think to themselves: 'You should have known better. If you can't choose good stocks, it's your fault,' said Morgan.

"Ug, yeah, I hid my stock market losses from my parents while in my senior year in high school. I took nine hundred dollars meant for my college fund and gambled it away based on a so-called great stock tip. I wanted to punch someone in the face for screwing me up." said Will.

"We despise the faults of others for what we see in ourselves. Our dark side makes us judge others harshly or sabotage them rather than help them view their mistakes with compassion. So everyone suffers in silence."

"You can see why we don't want to be vulnerable to ask for help. The greed and jealousy of humankind thrive on the guilty secrets of the uninformed who struggle to build their lives."

"Oh. How is the industry in trouble when bankers are making huge profits?" asked Will.

"The finance industry may decline into chaos through misbehaving investors, toothless governments & aging populations demanding support. **We have turned the boring concept of long term investing in blue-chip companies for retirement into a fast & quick casino gambling type of money management. In a zero-sum game, most do not have the expertise to make the right financial decisions to get the profits required for a comfortable retirement.**"

"Savers are looking to retire wealthy for a thirty-year holiday, so they are demanding very high returns. Salespeople are fickle and soft, so they show the best performing investments of the past and sell clients to believe that these outstanding returns will continue for a long time. Of course, this rarely happens."

"Investing is very confusing and frightening for some. People are reactive and short-sighted, so if they see poor returns in the first reporting cycle, they quit. Either they vacate the stock market and become very conservative in their savings or jump from one hot stock or fund to another. Many have neither the temperament nor the expertise to make good decisions."

"Wait a minute. Companies are no longer offering pension plans. We have to choose our own savings vehicle in a retirement plan through our companies. There is no choice but to go through a local retirement planner," said Will.

"Exactly. Retirement planning is like swimming among sharks with bleeding & exposed wounds. Your money is going to be someone's lunch. Many cunning and maleficent brokers will put their clients into really terrible investments that will give them the lion's share of the returns.[xcvi] If you find a good advisor, you are luckier than most. Remember, the broker gets paid first, no matter how well or poorly the investment does."

"Governments around the world have betrayed the public by turning a blind eye to the chaotic maelstrom in our financial system. Schools & colleges provide little to no monetary management training, and financial institutions benefit from keeping their clients in the dark. We already discussed how corporations induce political parties to write laws that benefit them and not the public."

"If companies use insider trading and buy stocks before the public learns the full picture, authorities have imprisoned very few executives. If firms engage in currency speculation and damage entire economies, regulators prosecute virtually no one. When corporations buy and sell risky stocks by deceiving investors about the creditworthiness, maybe their fines and penalties will be a fraction of what they steal from the public. It's a mess."

An employee furiously mopping the last area of the floor looked up and told Will the restaurant was closing in five minutes. Will got up, gathered his things, and put on his coat & hat. Yep. Morgan disappeared again. Why did that guy keep doing that?

RULE OF PRINCIPLE 31: *Moral people are bound to make bad errors, no matter how much they try to avoid mistakes. Please don't reject your humanity with all its flaws in search of perfectionism. Don't turn your mistakes into shame.*

Even if you have done a bad thing, your actions do not make you a defective person. You are a rational person who did an immoral thing. Guilt reminds you to do better next time. Please do not feel shame for your failings because it is a form of self-destruction that steals your peace of mind.

48. Night 17- FAMILY

The middle-aged couple expressed concern over their son's drained pallor. Is he on drugs? They whispered between the two of them.

Will convinced his parents that he was not sleeping well over the last few weeks due to overwork. He dreamt up a white lie to them that his project was taking up most evenings and weekends. In reality, he was struggling to fill up his regular nine to five hours with time-wasting chores & meetings.

In no way he would tell mom and dad that he was talking to a hallucination and driving around alone after midnight. Nor did he want to get their hope up by mentioning Angel.

Will's mother, Katherine, had made homemade meatloaf and mashed potatoes. The three of them sat around the old fashioned oak dining table set with her best silverware and china plates. Bill, his father, was also an engineer in electrical utilities. He explained to Will about the grid's growing expansion to power all the new housing developments popping up.

From observing his parents, he could see how magnificent life could be with a person to love. It confounded him how millions refused to get out of their comfort zones to explore the world to find their perfect match.

He did not want to be there. He liked his parents and spending time with them but desired rest rather than family.

The Sunday meal was usually delicious - this time, it tasted like cardboard paper, and he nibbled around the edges, waiting for the hour to be up.

49. Gambling - Don't Tempt Friends Into Harmful Diversions

As Will exited the gas station, hand clutching his gas receipt and three lotto tickets, he found Morgan sitting on his BMW hood. No longer surprised by these sudden appearances, he nonchalantly gestured to his hallucination to get inside."

The car sped off down the road and back onto the onramp of the highway. Morgan played with the radio as Will maneuvered back into the fast lane. Then they both reached to turn the radio off and laughed together at this unspoken agreement for quiet.

"Do you know why the dark side destroys lives even though there is all the information, scribes, coaches, therapists, monks, and shaman resources that almost anyone can tap into to have a wonderful life?"

"Because it is a terrible construction of the mind, God has bestowed us in payment for all our sins?" Will quipped.

"Ah, a man who knows a little of the Old Testament. No, people destroy themselves because they are ruled by their emotions and avoid using analytical knowledge from psychology and philosophy to make better decisions. People use wild strategies to avoid the pain of growth by suppressing their true feelings and indulging in pleasurable distractions[xcvii]."

"Many can't accept that life is difficult. We reject the problems in front of us and complain about them or ask others to fix them instead of doing it ourselves. When people mistake pleasure for happiness, they will find themselves on a roller coaster of drama and regret that never reaches any stopping point."

"I am confused. Are you saying people chase pleasure to avoid their problems? They don't know how to defeat our dark side?" asked Will.

"You can't defeat your dark side.[xcviii] You can only come to terms that it exists & then starve it of negative inputs. **There are many types of people and organizations that know how to push your pleasure buttons and get you hooked on addictive behaviors that will start you feeling high but will make you even more depressed, anxious and fearful.**"

Will questioned his teacher: "What's that? Drugs? Gambling? Shopping?"

"Gambling. Lottery corporations worldwide know their product is selling false dreams to people hungry to escape their poverty. We know a sizable one in fifty players are compulsive gamblers, yet governments are developing more casinos and lotto booths everywhere to rake in easy cash.

"The serious gamblers will spend all the cash they have and even cash advance on credit cards to pay for that irresistible high they get from a winning hand."

"You can dream of winning large jackpots of instant cash, which fuels future fantasies of a better lifestyle. Even small wins are pleasurable. It keeps you playing in anticipation of the big win, and that can be as fun as winning the jackpot itself."

"Adults who keep a budget to spend ten to twenty dollars per week on the lottery don't realize that they may waste an average of $20,000 to $50,000 over their lifetimes on a game that only six to eight hundred Americans will win (grand prize jackpots) each year."

"Compulsive casino gamblers may spend enormous quantities of money chasing that high. Even after the game playing becomes boring and mundane, addicts feel no more pleasure from it but can also get little enjoyment from anything else."

"I understand because external goals like making money, partying, or becoming popular never ends. Gamblers are never pleased because they want to win even more money once their feelings of euphoria are gone. Do these gambling addicts lead normal lives and have jobs, families, and hobbies?" asked Will.

"Normal lives full of frustration, grief, sadness, loneliness, guilt, regret, fear, and despair. You know a life free of addiction is difficult enough. Imagine adding gambling to all the other problems. Addicts feel like they have no discipline to control themselves and feel like a leaf blowing in the wind."

"Unbridled recklessness is also caused by players having a lack of long-term perspective. Rather than hearing that the odds of winning the top prize are one in ten million, they hear "anyone can win." Even if you tell players the facts about winning or the horror stories of lotto winners, they regularly play. The enjoyment of fantasizing about spending millions of dollars & having a good time is too irresistible a lure."

"The reality is that the group that plays the most also has the worst spending and saving habits. They don't know how to invest or budget, so those few who win will blow most of it on big houses, stupid trips, expensive cars, and helping out relatives. Seventy percent of winners spend all their lotto money within five years.[xcix]"

"And the lotto executives know this? Millions of people waste money on a false pleasure that has little chance of payout?. Half the winners go bankrupt. How can they live with themselves knowing they are causing anxiety, fear, worry, and depression in the population?" asked Will

"Rationalization. The gambling chiefs can weigh this damning evidence against the benefits of all sorts of a restaurant, entertainment, and construction jobs. They will say most people do not get addicted and find betting a nice night out with friends. That is true, but don't tell me gambling resorts are the only ways to create jobs and entertainment."

"Yes, the corporations and illegal gangs running betting tracks, casinos, and lotto games know their customers' psychology better than the players themselves." They see the same faces every week. These addicts are the source of most of their profits."

"It brings in tax dollars. That's the logical argument. I don't buy that nonsense. Those who profit from this industry are like everyone else. They get hooked on the 'thrill of the chase and kill.' They can't stop exploiting their customers in the same way gamblers can't quit placing bets."

RULE OF PRINCIPLE 32: *Be compassionate about the addictions, poverty, and feeble judgment of others, and perhaps you shall acquire a strange peace of mind extremists lack. It is impossible not to judge others, so when you can, think of them favorably. When you view strangers or friends positively, they can feel it and may do the same to you. Moral superiority is an illusion. Even if you are measurably better than others in your conduct, friendship loss creates an impoverished life.*

50. Conservatism - Start Small & Help Open Minded Individuals

"What else did you want to talk about today?" asked Will

"One other thing before I get started. Why do you think I am telling you about all sorts of nasty behavior in a wide variety of industries?"

Will was a little bleak, "That the world is a horrible place full of thieves and conmen? I should not trust anyone and protect myself at all times?"

"If you believe that, I have failed you as a teacher. Did we not talk about humanity's light side as well?"

"Anxious students look at the dark side of society and fear to challenge it. They throw up their hands and complain that nothing can be done. They are wrong!"

"If you want your world to get better, you need to take action in places where corrupt devils are used to seeing weakness. Accustomed to passivity; they don't expect real fighters to stand and demand higher moral standards than we have fallen to."

"You have got to understand your enemy, not just so you can avoid him, but so you can outsmart his cunning manipulation. Throughout the centuries, workers recapitulated to authorities, to be run over and exploited right until death because they were unaware of the game's rules.

"I want you to understand a few more of the unwritten rules that are missing from your Lifebook, so you can fully participate, thrive, and win in this new, brutally competitive environment."

"I don't desire your transformation from a young man, experimenting with life's adventures into a cynical, tired elitist who is fearful of change. Someone who will bend the rules of decency because his dogmatic rigidity sees threats from younger generations striving for goals very different from his own."

"Okay, fine. I think this exhaustion is making me pessimistic. Of course, I want to keep up a positive attitude." defended Will.

"Don't be too positive, and don't be too negative. Be prepared & plan for the best outcomes possible."

"Millions of people engage in magical thinking. They feel that somehow everything will work out. They spend freely and say yes to many people and opportunities all the time without preparing for these challenges. This impulsive naivety attracts predators who seek to take advantage of them."

"A second group has lost all faith in humanity. Their existence is dank, dark, and depressing because they are too afraid to venture out and experiment. Every person unknown is a threat. All opportunities are potential scams. They believe anyone who became successful must have schemed and conned their way out by stealing. With such a negative attitude, they sink further and further into the poverty of the mind. Being of this mindset is also a mistake."

"Then the realists: Most of humanity does not dare to confront dangerous tasks, a natural survival mechanism built into our DNA. We stare at problems from a distance and hope they will go away. Our dark side makes us cower in fear, put on a brave front, and then these assertive business leaders swoop in, solve the problem, and take the lions' share of, well, everything. "

"While realists can move brilliantly, they too have blind spots that hinder them from seeing their weaknesses and the repercussions of their actions. Avoid this group too."

"Well, that does not help. Isn't that everyone in the world?" Will wanted clarification.

"There are a few business owners and professionals who believe in more than making a buck and having fun. The excuse 'It was just business' is not an acceptable rationale for deceiving customers, cheating suppliers, or mistreating workers."

"Moral leaders want to work, leave a legacy, and be someone. 'That was a good person' mourners would proclaim after they pass on. They can foresee the rotten and corrupt ideas in their fellow citizens' minds and still cordially work together in pursuit of the greater good. These are the types of people you should emulate."

"Ahh, I don't know if I could live up to those expectations. I am just an employee." Will rejected the idea.

"No pressure, Will. No one is asking you to turn into Gandhi overnight. Just try to do a little better every day and slowly but surely you will, at the minimum, be able to sleep at night, secure that you did the right thing when it counted."

"Oh, yes, that reminds me. If you want to be of a high moral character, do not attack or argue with people who have contrary belief systems. That means do not insult conservatives if you are liberal, do not slam men if you are a woman, do not say Eastern religion is strange if you are Christian. And so on. You understand why?"

"Because you can lead a horse to water but can't make her drink?" Will quipped.

"That is funny. A smartass, eh? It is indeed impossible to change another person's personal beliefs through pure logic and rationality. You are inviting conflict within and all around you."

"The main reason to do so is that it is disrespectful and ignorant to offend others' customs and culture even if they share the same language, work, and nationality. In turn, others may return respect for your values to you."

"All these fights on social media about protests, politics, and gender equality are in poor taste. Much of it is simple and unrefined, and neither side will comprehend they are fueling the arguments as much as the opposition. Go ahead, Will. If you want more negativity, anger, and frustration in your life, spend your nights debating the far-right conservatives. See how much happier you will be in a year!"

"No, no, no. That is not for me," Will agreed.

"Good, now since you are a progressive person who believes in free expression, government regulation, and environmental protection, we can talk about how to understand conservatives."

"Traditionalists or conservatives believe in established institutions like schools, military, religion, family, and prisons. Many, if not most, prefer fixed rules, harsh punishments, conformity, masculine dominance, nuclear families, closed borders, small-town values, and law & order."

"Some of this is healthy because some of these values establish the stability civilizations require for vibrant commerce, peace, and harmony. The problem with traditionalists is that they are reluctant to embrace new ideas, cultures, and activities. Imagine older people who still have rotary or flip phones, clothing from the eighties, eat meat and potatoes every other day, and vote Republican no matter how bad the candidate."

"Democrats and liberals are making a big mistake if they think they can explain their policies and values to conservatives, and persuade them to change their minds."

"Yes, many traditionalists do not understand the issues. No, it is very tough to influence them to switch positions. Their mindset is fixed and firm. They will refuse to see the light even if you pile on the evidence to the contrary."

"Where are you going with this?" the young man asked.

"We don't know why conservatives, more than liberals, see the world as a dangerous and threatening place, engulfed by the disorder & chaos of liberal conceptions[c]. Maybe it was their strict upbringing, abuse from other children, physical punishment, the indoctrination of schooling, or the dark message of religion. I don't know."

"The goals of the wealthy and conservatives are aligned in the same direction—neither desire to change as proposed by our liberal scientists & philosophers. The rich, who are often elderly and conservative themselves, want to continue to accumulate their wealth without the threat of tax or redistribution. Conservatives are just afraid of many things they have not found to be safe."

"Here is where politics become evil and malicious. Many politicians, representing the elite one percent, amplify these threats traditionalists fear by misrepresenting the intentions of all those outside the conservative movement."

"Yeah, I knew that. Politicians do scare the hell out of voters to get elected. You believe that to be an atrocious act of selfishness?"

"It is. The wealthy are playing the anger, frustration, and insecurities of both liberal and conservative taxpayers against each other, driving a wedge of abusive conflict in between them and looting and exploiting their country's resources as it happens."

"Are you talking about the divide and conquer strategy of war? What if the two sides worked out their differences?" Will asked.

"It might help a little, but you can't solve this underlying emotional fear of conservatives with rational & logical arguments."

"But these conservatives are working in innovative careers, using modern medicine and the latest computer technology." Will pushed back.

"None of these tools threatens the traditionalist's core beliefs the way challenging crises in institutions like work, school, religion & law has. As I said, you can't solve heartfelt terror with objective, coherent evidence."

"But if we use education..."

"The dark side of a traditionalist will overwhelm his mind with a thundering of anger, anxiety, and fear to drown out the sound of wisdom. "

Will was disappointed. "So that is it. There is no good solution, eh?"

"I don't want this narrative to sound like an attack on the fifteen to twenty percent who are staunch conservatives. Humanity's slow march of progress has depended on the hard work of conservative stewardship, with the stimulus of liberal philosophy propelling us forward on occasion."

"Despite all the conflict, liberals and conservatives need each other to keep the world running smoothly. Yet, there is a danger if traditional doctrine consumed the totality of liberal ideology..."

"What's that?" he asked.

"Nothing

Conservatives desire to suppress revolutionary thoughts and non-conforming ideas at all costs.

No laws &

Abolition means banning sexual images, alternative lifestyles, & nontraditional partnerships

No military actions

Block reproductive, children, or LGBTQ rights, & allow capital punishment for cultural offenses.

Wili dislodge the

Defund the free press, investigative journalism, & experimental art.

Subconscious anxiety

Deregulate businesses, pollution management, & workers' rights.

That the outside world is

Chop government programs, defund welfare, & overfund churches into power centers.

Insecure or unsafe

Demand conformity in speech, clothing, and values, so everyone acts and behaves the same."

"In short, traditionalists want to build a metaphorical fort with high walls to protect themselves. For liberals, that society would be a prison. A miserable experience for both sides because conservative philosophies will solve neither conflict nor insecurity to the satisfaction of all."

"Virtually nobody is pointing out that today's Conservatives were yesterday's Liberals. Evangelical Christians would be considered heretical revolutionaries by members of the

Roman Empire. Advocates of government-run police forces, armies & free speech rights would be deemed left-wing savages by the Kings & Queens of medieval Europe."

"So, there is always hope that even entrenched conservatives will eventually adopt some of the ideas they passionately resist today."

"Before you decide to feel superior with your progressive ideology, remember Liberals have their fatal flaws. They are so open-minded & accommodating next to stern conservative; it takes them an extremely long time to organize and make decisions. If pure Liberals ran things, well, it might not be socialism, but high taxes, complex regulation, and widespread poverty might rule the day. Liberals need conservatives to help them run the day to day operations."

"This is a fairly exhausting topic! We are almost home. Am I going to get some real sleep tonight? Please tell me something good? Please?" Will begged.

"What do you think? Will? He answered cryptically

It was going to be another long night.

RULE OF PRINCIPLE 33: Please *don't be weak but also don't be a reckless instigator of ill conceived ideas. Be strategic in your activism. Passively sitting by while people are being manipulated and controlled by forces you understand, and they don't, is the wrong thing to do. Challenging the status quo by directly attacking institutions and values is a mistake. You will invite many conflicts into your life. Instead, create a counterculture and ask like-minded activists to join.*

51. Night 18 - EVASIVE

Will called the blonde to ask if she wanted to go ice skating and then get some spicy Italian pasta dinner with him.

Maybe they could do that soon, but Angel was not in the mood at the moment. Ask her in a few days. She softened the blow of rejection.

An awkward silence filled the air. The couple did not know what to say next. Angel changed the subject by telling Will about a new jacket and skirt she just bought online.

Will teased her about her purchase. He said he liked it when she got dressed up fancy but preferred it when she stripped for him. He hoped to see that outfit on her sexy little body and then later on the floor.

That set her off in a flurry of giggling. Angel was the window into a world of playfulness, where they could chase each other and have tickle fights and not care that children without jobs and responsibilities loved such silliness.

Looking back on their romance, Will remembered the time he demanded to know how good a lover he was. She was evasive about ranking him among all her old boyfriends. But Angel did say something that he never heard from a woman before:

She said to him years ago. You are sweet without being weak. That is a rare combination. Some guys are nice all the time, and they never say no to me. Other guys are rough and inconsiderate. They expect me to follow without asking me. You ask for my opinion. You charge ahead without hesitation. You lead when we go out. I like that you say no more than yes while you open doors for me. I prefer strong character more than diamonds, lobster, champagne, and Ferraris.

Hello? Angel's voice broke through and interrupted his memories. She demanded why he was not paying attention to her. He had drifted off into his thoughts. Finally, Will confesses that he had insomnia. This lack of sleep was dulling his senses, so he had trouble concentrating. She had no right answers for him, so she wished him a good night's sleep and hung up.

52. Join Revolutionary Forces Outside Political Arenas, Not Within

"Why do you dislike your political leaders, Will? Are there any politicians that you especially hate?" asked Morgan.

The two men were outside. When Will could not sleep, a night time walk helped him escape his claustrophobic conditions. Morgan seemed to show up whenever Will began to forget about him.

He thought quickly, "My state senator is pretty terrible. His party thinks they are rationally sound, but they are enacting laws and policies that create chaos, corruption, and inefficiencies."

"What types of laws were terrible?" Morgan asked again.

"They cut tax funding for some highways and bridges and installed expensive toll routes on the best roads. Now the free highways are deteriorating and more congested than ever. The toll highways are underutilized because many drivers can't afford them," Will explained.

"This traffic problem is a symptom of a greater dilemma. The politicians who go the furthest are not the practical, number crunchers who can keep budgets under control but can tell stories of things we worship even if it goes against the community.[ci] Through social media, television ads, and news interviews, persuasive leaders can exploit our emotions and control what we think about."

247

"They misuse our attraction to family values, nationalism, celebrity worship, and wealth creation to distract us from seeing the true power dynamics. Politicians ignore widespread poverty, infrastructure budgets, education reform, and environmentalism because they are too damn difficult to solve."

"We want simple stories that make us feel good, and our dark side makes us act emotional when the wisest course to think logically.[cii] It's often leaders with the darkest auras who are most skilled at weaving manipulative stories that make us seem empowered."

"I get it. By transforming themselves into someone of power and influence who entertains rather than solve issues, politicians can avoid working on long term problems that need recognition but don't attract donors or votes," said Will.

"Exactly, we are creating a culture that prefers distraction and entertainment than dealing with truly chronic issues that need attention. This disloyalty to the very institutions they have pledged their allegiance produces token legislation designed to keep them in power."

"In a system where the public is bored and uninterested, and the two or three main political parties fight to the draw in terms of supporters and funding very little transpires. Endless campaigning and elections become the main job of the legislative system, not passing laws."

"Thus, all the poverty, educational & environmental problems that lack advocates are neglected in favor of lobby groups that trade campaign donations for political favors[ciii]."

"So our political system is breaking down because our leaders are the most charismatic and not the most competent? I don't know. Some politicians have, like, no personality at all." said Will

"No matter what system of government (parliamentary, republic, socialist, autocratic), the most sweeping problem is that those who have the greatest skills at convincing others they should lead are often the worst managers of political resources."

"Is the corruption of politics due to neglect or deliberate sabotage?" asked Will.

"Often the candidate with the wealthiest backers wins elections. Most large businesses do not want to support officers who want to raise taxes, protect the environment, or strengthen workers' rights. Corporate interests will throw buckets of money at the politicians who help perpetuate conditions where owners maintain their stranglehold on the economy."

"Thus the most corruptible, dishonest power-hungry social climbers can find work in politics blocking any positive change that the "do-gooder" leaders want to push through."

"Even if a sizable portion of a nation or community demands urgent changes and elects their champions to office, the other politicians are backed by conservative voters or business elites. This tug of war is enough to block most laws that could profoundly transform society and government."

Will and Morgan continued walking briskly through the sleet and slush. They had already traversed six city blocks.

"Many voters believe that politics has nothing to do with them, their careers, or their family life. Some want to blow the system up and replace it with anarchy, fascism, authoritarianism, or communism. These are all foolish ideas."

"Poor leadership creates a vacuum of inspiration, and many citizens feel disinherited, alienated, and disappointed. Failed policies make us lose faith in our institutions and the system of democracy itself. We demand new leadership, and it's going to evolve from grass-roots organizations, not establishment political parties."

"That is yet another problem with the educational system. Many nations & empires have tried different forms of government and failed to make progress. Experimenting with these alternatives to democracy have all inflicted massive misery on the populace."

"Instructors teach history but don't explain to high school students why democracy is the only viable way to transfer power without using violence or the sacrifices made to establish this peaceful governance."

RULE OF PRINCIPLE 34: *Too many leaders gain power by attacking the other side. Assigning blame is effective but allows inactivity, stagnation, and corruption because time spent attacking is time wasted building. It's a terrible act to attack vulnerable groups to gain or maintain power. Please don't do it. You are spreading blame and hate among the populations in ways that are as damaging as vandalism & crime.*

53. Education - Schools Do Not Teach The Wisdom Necessary For Transformation

Morgan rounded the corner, and Will followed him. He wondered if these stories were relevant to his life? Was he learning anything valuable?

"It is very apparent to many business leaders and educators that most countries' public education system is wholly outdated for a world with artificial intelligence, robotics, bio-engineering, and virtual reality."

"Most schools fail to prepare students for life beyond childhood. They give children literacy and take away agency. Instead of teaching students how to become independent thinkers who can solve work, family, and life problems freely, they install ideas of obedience, conformity, and follower thinking.[civ]"

"Before I start, I must state it's not completely fair to lay the blame on the modern education system. Many parents fail to provide basic social skills that are necessary to do well even before the child steps into his or her first class."

"Transforming children into respectable members of society who could follow the rules and accept structured work hours and tasks without question made sense in the industrial age. You could make a living as a cog in the machine or as a labor input in factories so long as most laborers were systemized, routine, and manual."

"Going forward, manufacturers and even service industries may find it much more profitable in the future to lease robots and computer networks than to hire humans. People may not be needed to serve food, cook meals, clean homes, drive vehicles, stock shelves, tend to children, and perform many low skill tasks."

"As technology decimates the labor force, employees require better skills to negotiate salaries, re-educate themselves, move to places of opportunity, and maybe even start new businesses."

"Learning how to follow instructions, wait for management decisions, and specialize in very narrow professions damages independent thinking.[cv] When you rely on others to create work for you, they decide who receives the most significant share of profits, not you. As an employee, your income is more dependent on the whims of the free labor market than if you were a business owner."

"Are professionals like accounting, law, medicine, and engineering under threat from this technological change?" asked Will.

"Very difficult to predict. Based on recent events, we can visualize a world where almost any job or career can be performed better by a computer than a human."

"It's not just about jobs and careers. Traditional classroom education from kindergarten through grade twelve encourages shadow behavior. Instead of learning how to become superior, wiser & happier human workers, the rote memorization of mathematics, grammar, biology, and civics teach our best children to become grade seeking conformists."

Will asked, "How?"

"Education also teaches a sizable portion of students to hate learning. They struggle to learn, become functionally illiterate, and drop out of school, cutting themselves off from the rich possibilities of life.

"Okay, How?" Will repeated.

"Guess what happens when the dark side of the shadow comes in contact with such a rigid, inflexible, and cruel system?" Morgan asked rhetorically.

"Children are learning emotional and intellectual intelligence at different rates, even within the same grade. Some aggressive children learn how to manipulate, intimidate, or hurt slower classmates who are not at their level.[cvi] Remarkable students learn it is safer not to reveal superior intelligence for fear of being ridiculed, while slower students present a false front that they comprehend the material taught."

"Amid conformity, some kids have interests and hobbies that are considered unpopular, so successful students shun them until they switch to activities that are considered cool.[cvii] Popular kids establish a pecking order, and their followers enforce these unwritten rules. All this happens between and after classes."

"Children have to navigate a minefield of emotions while growing up all while trying to learn how to choose a career, apply to college, date, get good grades, and all the other pressures of pre-teen and teen life. Many students, for a wide variety of reasons, don't fit in. Their grades drop, they self-isolate, avoid friends that aren't understanding and generally develop into unhealthy, poorly-adjusted adults.[cviii]"

"When you put children in a system designed for others but not for them, you are strengthening their shadow. Bad teachers, bullies, and unhealthy relationships based on popularity and reputation all create stress and anxiety for very intelligent but misunderstood teens."

"These children feel guilty about performing poorly and blame themselves. Struggling students can see other kids thrive in this environment, so they believe there must be something wrong with them. They hide their greatness, sweetness, and authentic personality by disconnecting from their true (but unpopular) talents and feel underappreciated, foolish, stupid, and even nihilistic.[cix]"

"Are you telling me the education system is defective, and it's not the students' fault?" Will asked.

"Teaching is a noble and challenging profession, but instructional institutions are as non-compassionate and mechanistic as the corporate world it is beholden.

Education's goal is to transform children into workers, separating A students to a professional track, B & C students to support staff & trades, and failing students into unskilled work or the welfare system."

"Within classes, those students with the visual ability to concentrate, memorize, and read well receive notice from their teachers, and they earn better grades than neglected students who fall further behind. Children with learning disabilities auditory strengths, artistic abilities can't compete."

"Many students can learn best through auditory listening or using their hands and body, but schools require them to use their eyes to memorize the notes on blackboards or study their textbooks. The ones with strong visual & language skills graduate with higher grades because they thrive in this 3R (wRiting, Reading, aRithmetic) system."

"The same system designed to liberate minds and expand horizons entraps both pupils and educators. Can't you see that schools have always been 'dressed up' assembly lines intended to manufacture a new supply of compliant employees? That the interests of the system and students run contrary to each other?"

"As the employers' ratchet up their demands for more sophisticated workers, parents and students are scrambling to make sure they are on 'A' conveyor belt headed for college. While families hire tutors, move to live near the right schools, and take on extra-curricular activities, teachers either endure this madness by focusing on their best scholars or live in resignation, trying to attend to as many students as time allows.[cx]"

"As children progress, taxpayers and politicians all have varying, contradictory ideas and beliefs about how kids should learn and what they should learn. Educators who try new techniques or request changes to subject matters often get frozen out or fired, so conservatism tends to dominate the system. Education organized around a society that existed two hundred years ago is stubborn to change."

"Okay, we are almost home." said Will.

"One last thing," Morgan said as he left Will at the door. "There is a decades-long battle between established teachers who love the profession, think education works fine, and believe bad students are lazy & disciplined, and idealistic educators."

"The second group likes teaching, recognizes classroom struggles but does not know how to bust old traditions, or are too exhausted to help D & F students. Some teachers are terrible, someone should fire them, but it's chiefly the system that can't recognize different learning styles that require innovative teaching methods."

RULE OF PRINCIPLE 35: *If you are a parent, academic education is utterly inadequate for your child's needs - they must continue to learn social, dating, parental, leadership, and business skills from kindergarten to the age of retirement. If they are a poor student, do not medicate them or punish them as a knee jerk reaction, maybe it's the school and not them. Determine their learning style and find a teaching environment that works best for the artistic, creative, sports-oriented, hyperactive students who struggle with writing & memorization.*

Your children are not clones of you or property that you own. Do not try to remake them in your image and force them to adopt careers and lifestyles that they do not want. Be their guardian, mentor & teacher so they can choose their values, beliefs, and goals.

54. Night 19 - HUNGER

Was this the purpose of real life? Will was staring at a mobile phone screen in his BMW, waiting for responses from friends. Some random Facebook friends replied to his messages, but none of them were the ones he wanted for conversation.

Was Angel so busy that she could not give him a few seconds to reply? He assumed that she was playing games with him, dangling him along until all her other friends bored her, and she turned to him for entertainment.

Vapid messages bombarded girls like her so that they were spending hours just receiving empty validation from admirers and frenemies climbing the social ladder. He hated her for falling back into this social noise and loved her when she turned it off to give him the attention he craved.

The apartment felt alone without a feminine presence. The bachelor could not bear to drive home until the placid city turned off its lights and forced him back to his quiet apartment.

Finally, at 10:30 pm, Angel sent a brief smiley face text. Will sent her a sarcastic message in reply; I was thrilled being miserable until you came back into my life and ruined it.

Well, you are both the pin and the cushion for my backside, she teased back. Do you mean you want to sit on me? Will questioned her. No, stupid, you give me all the support I need, but sometimes you can be a real pain in the ass, the blonde replied.

55. Warfare - War Is State Sanctioned Murder Supported By Xenophobia

It was midnight and with no luck falling asleep, Will decided to drive to the waterfront. He was always fascinated with Navy frigates and aircraft carriers. There were a couple of small support ships docked at the harbor.

Under the dark winter night, the Navy abandoned the docks till morning. The rest of the tourists and sailors would not return for several weeks when the weather warmed up.

Will pulled into a parking lot spot closest to the nearest boat and turned off his lights. As his eyes adjusted to the lights' glare coming off the ships, he saw Morgan standing near the gangplank looking up at the captain's command center.

"Hello. I wonder how you found me?" Will asked.

"Oh, hello Will. You know that wherever you go, I come with you."

The two men began walking through the snow along the pier, looking at the few remaining boats moored, not dry-docked for winter. They picked up the pace when the wind decided to harass them with a pounding force.

"You understand that humanity is not a 'us and them' situation. You can't always say that person belongs in a group of good people and that another person belongs in that bad group. It's not that simple. We are all prone to tribalism, hypocritical thinking, and dark thoughts that make the average person break rules in some situations and adhere to them in other places."

"Yes, we all have some good and some evil in us, and it's our responsibility to be a person of high character so we can construct the life we want," replied Will.

"Definitely. You make your individualized heaven or hell. It starts in your mind. If you march into hell like the soldiers and civilians of WWII had to endure, then it's on you to see the good in people when they reveal their true nature."

"The madness of war causes soldiers to dehumanize their enemies as not worthy of respect or life itself. But people do not commit rape, assault, and killings in large numbers for enjoyment and pleasure. This primate fear of outsiders taking away food and resources triggers a fit of anger inside and causes some of the more violent to express their rage."

"The military trains soldiers to obey orders, right? They don't allow their soldiers to kill and rape if they have secured the fighting zone." Will pushed back.

"The generals and military structure in most historical armies silently condone and even encourage this vilest behavior because terrorism of a population is a proven war strategy that can be very effective at demoralizing populations."

"Recent international laws and greater human rights activism make this less common, but the lack of journalists and public advocates in war/conflict zones make it possible for the most brutal soldiers to rape and assault the enemy without penalty. War can turn into state-sanctioned murder, so some thrill-seeking males choose to become soldiers to get the opportunity to exercise the godlike power of death on people they learned to hate."

'That's sick. I don't believe it." said Will

"Remember, most soldiers strive to fight for their country and go home—the vast majority. You will see platoons accepting the enemy's surrender without violence and escorting them safely to the war camps. There are countless stories of American and British soldiers giving some of their food rations to starving families in Europe. War brings out the best and worst of us."

"Okay, okay. I want to hear about those rapists and murderous soldiers. How did they get accepted into the armed forces?" asked Will.

"These malicious and vindictive soldiers were prone to violence from a young age. They were difficult to raise. Often got in trouble at school. Refused to obey instructions. Then some adapted and learned how to avoid punishment while retaining their rebelliousness."

"While pretending to follow the rules, they would bully other children. They took this malice, spiteful, and hateful nature and made blunt calculations when to be aggressive and when not to be.[cxi] Their parents neglected to teach sympathy and caring for others, so they never had a chance. Bullying gave these aggressive children the feeling of high status and power, and they leaned into it."

"What's the connection between bullying and becoming a killer?" asked Will

"This ignorance of the other-self, the positive & kind person they could be, fueled their bigotry, hatred, and prejudices. Circumstances extinguished the spark of goodness in them, and gaining pleasure from others' pain became a game they enjoyed the most. Their vindictive nature made them seek revenge against anyone who hurt them."

 "And when the soldier got his first kill, he was on the path to destruction and mayhem." offered Will.

"Back into hell. Humans can be tough, but this type of malevolence can break the spirit in ways earthquakes, famine, and floods cannot. Unleashing these types of monsters brings misery to innocents, and this tragedy can shake generations of family lineage before they come back into the light."

"I have rarely been a supporter of conflict, but this makes me want to protest any political movements that encourage armed forces. The risks of turning hostile nations into killing fields are just too great," stated Will.

RULE OF PRINCIPLE 36: *Real war is more horrific than in video games or in the movies, watching friends and civilians die may give you nightmares. Do not take up arms and go to war by invading another country. Your government has failed you if they could not negotiate diplomatic terms peacefully. If a foreign invader attacks, you can defend your own home or city with firearms, but when you go to another country to kill, that is state-sanctioned murder.*

56. War Hawks - Do Not Profit From War Or You Will Root Against Peace

Will and his imaginary friend got back into the warm shelter of the BMW. He cranked up the heater and rubbed his hand together to warm up.

"War is not only self-destructive for soldiers and civilians, but it is also a waste of resources like military equipment, crops, natural resources, buildings, and land. Combat rarely resolves itself quickly with a decisive victory."

The victor has to expend a tremendous amount of workforce managing and suppressing the angry and unruly opposition. After years of civil war, those in power who negotiate peace terms end up being just as corrupt and tyrannical as the autocrats they replaced."

"All wars start in the minds of those that have conceived of them. We are impressive in our capacity to invent stories and deceive ourselves into believing them to be true. All conflicts are from taking our lies to their violent extreme."

"As humans are natural-born liars, we learn how much power is in the lie. This internal struggle to distinguish my lie from your lie makes us experiment and push the bounds of decency and integrity. With guidance from experienced mentors, some learn that lying for gain is too costly a price, while their opponents see great value in taking lies and marshaling resources to fight a common enemy."

"My head is spinning. Lying leads to war? Something is missing here. Wars cost resources like money and soldiers but don't the winner take all of the loser's wealth and pay for what was lost? I thought some war parties or countries make money from having wars." asked Will

"That's the larger deception we are discussing. War is a horrific game of risk and reward. If you can gain more than you lose, it may be worth the gamble." In reality, most wars end with a stalemate, or the victor loses vast capital resources; they would have been better off not fighting at all."

"Many rebel forces in civil hostilities are funded by other governments and interested parties who can get favorable trade deals if they win. Very few members of the public understand who the players are or what they want. They know that the ethnic group they dislike is on another side and their family and neighbors are on the side they want to win. Soldiers and the public are manipulated by political leaders to fight the opposing side at great cost."

"If the war is between two countries, armies destroy thousands of acres of farmland, thousands or millions of soldiers die or are injured, and the populations of both countries grow increasingly distressed and xenophobic about the other side."

"Certain families & organizations know exactly how to make huge fortunes by selling arms, speculating in investments, and buying and selling resources no

matter who wins. It is in their interests to set the deception in motion."

"Okay, so almost everyone loses by participating in a war, willingly or unwillingly. How does lying cause our dark sides to desire war?"

"That's a little backward. Our blackened souls desire war and conflict, so we invent lies to make them come to fruition. There is a force so hateful of love and all that is good; it seeks the destruction of humanity."

"It makes us forget who we are and what amazing inventions can arise out of great minds. We can't remember we not only play by the rules; we make them as well. This collective force of the worst of humankind takes a strength that consumes all in its path."

"It deceives, enrages, and exhorts people to abandon reason and encircle themselves with anger, vengeance, hatred, and fear. If a sizable portion of the ruling elites accepts these lies, war starts."

"But…" Will began

"You want me to tell you when it is acceptable to defend yourself? Fine. If the enemy is at your doorstep and your allied forces are not there to guard you, you may protect yourself. Of course. There are times to be a pacifist and times to challenge your attacker. Fight to preserve your life, fight to protect your community, fight because it's your home, and no one has the right to take it away from you."

"USA! USA! USA!" Will chanted as Morgan gasped in surprise. "I am just messing with you. Of course, I agree with all you said. Our military might is so awesome, and I'm proud of that."

Morgan walked away into the mist, shaking his head. "The dark side is strong in this one. Maybe he is kind of hopeless."

"Hey, it was a joke, okay?" Will called out at the fleeting figure.

RULE OF PRINCIPLE 37: *Tame your dark side. Anger, hatred, envy, and fear start in the mind and spreads outward to your family and community. If you don't understand how to come to peace with the conflict within you, you will take your battles outside yourself to combat the people you love. A tranquil, safe community and a peaceful, kind world depend on its inhabitants maturing into wise, compassionate, and thoughtful adults who understand the impact of their actions on their surroundings.*

57. Night 20 - REINVIGORATE

Is it not surprising how a single random call in the early evening can change lives in very significant ways. The five civil engineers on the fourth floor had felt listless because their bosses suddenly withdrew from the previous project, leaving them to fill their days with busy work and silliness.

Will was a thoughtful person, and as he adjusted to learning about the new contract starting next week, he realized that there is no life without purpose. That is why the team atmosphere seemed depressing and unpleasant. They had nothing to live for at work if there weren't any challenging and exciting problems for them to solve.

He was about to send a flurry of texts to his team to let them know what was up. There was a knock on the apartment door that interrupted his purpose.

It was her. Angel. Even in a heavy parka coat and tight blue jeans tucked inside tall cowboy boots, she looked fantastic. She grabbed him in a bear hug and kissed him on the lips hard. Woah, he exclaimed, don't you want to romance me first?

Angel giggled and said no, she was not interested in talking tonight. She unzipped her coat, kicked off her boots, and took Will's hand, leading him to the bedroom.

58. Arms Manufacturers Fight Hard to Prevent Illegitimate Wars

He stared in delight at the topless woman on stage. She was grinding and swinging on a pole against the resounding noise of a club song. This place was gross and seedy. It was full of rough & quiet men who stared at this shimmering beauty as if she was a mirage in the desert.

No one was paying attention to him. The dark smoke obscured the patron's faces. A man no one saw sat down next in the chair next to Will. He whistled under his breath at the sexy woman in front and waited for the young man to acknowledge him.

Will exhaled out and asked Morgan his first question:

"Hi, Morgan. I have meant to ask you. Is there any man or woman in history who has eliminated their Shadow? Maybe the Dhali Lama, Moses, Abraham, or the Buddha?" asked Will.

"No, picture the kindest & most generous person in the world. He or she will have some small amount of envy, greed, or desire in their heart. If you ask if you can achieve some sort of transcendence awakening or enlightenment where you are free of your fears and sadness? Forget it. All of humanity has some dark side in them. No exceptions."

"The spark of both good and evil resides in the same heart that beats within. Are you willing to cut out your heart to destroy the devil inside? You cannot have good inside you without having the capacity for evil; otherwise, a decision no longer becomes a rational choice but something forced upon you by fate," said Morgan.

"Okay. I still believe we can improve ourselves so that we can reduce that negative chatter in our minds. Those voices that tell us we are failures or that we are unworthy of love and respect." said Will.

"Yes, you may believe that. Yes, you may attempt to live a life of purity, kindness, and wisdom so that you can look back on your deathbed with pride at what you have accomplished and all you have become."

"As we discussed before, there are many parties that desire war and conflict so that they may profit from them. The men who participate in such schemes have blackened hearts full of rage, destruction, fighting, and revenge. The biggest winners of war are the arms manufacturers who make handsome profits during peacetime and obscene profits during wars."

"They sound like real pieces of work. Is it just about profit, or is there more to it?" Will asked.

"Humans have a desire to create, but they also have a compulsion to destroy. War makes the dark side very powerful because the beneficiaries perceive like they are seizing back control in a chaotic world full of enemies and threats. There is nothing like the ability to send soldiers into war to die to make a leader feel like a God."

"That's despicable," he commented.

"As I said, politicians rationalize arms spending by telling their populace the nation must be ready for the potential of war. Many industrialists pay lobbyists in the capital to pressure politicians to take aggressive stands during times of hostility."

"The more criminally minded executives of gun, tank, and airplane manufacturers fund and support political candidates that are more war hawk than peace dove. In due time, these executives request big government contracts to earn dividends on those political contributions."

A sexy tiny black girl in white shorts and lacy bra came up to Will's table and asked him if he wanted a lapdance in the back room. Will declined, and she shuffled away in disappointment. Morgan resumed talking.

"When the authorities allow captains of industry to do just about what they want, some will commit unspeakable acts in the pursuit of power and profits."

"Arms manufacturers have been known to sell guns, planes, and tanks to hostile countries while publicly claiming to be patriotic and loyal to their home nations. They will also convince wealthy nations to fund civil war participants in low-income countries to sell the weapons to both revolutionaries and authoritarian regimes."

"Don't these people have any conscience? Are dollars worth more than human lives?" asked Will.

"Evil can become familiar with the right circumstances. Under the guise of being patriotic and job-creators, armament companies can convince enough voters to demand politicians keep these factories busy even during peace times. The armament industry has the opportunity to create all sorts of deadly forces that require men, machinery, capital, engineering, and fuel."

"So instead of dealing with widespread problems such as healthcare, education, infrastructure and crime that could employ hundreds of thousands of workers, governments fund military budgets that create fewer jobs and impoverish the nation," said Will.

"Fear and anxiety in those chasing power cause pain, death, and poverty for others."

RULE OF PRINCIPLE 38: *Avoid Fights & Arguments. When someone judges you harshly, gossips, or insults you, try to ignore them. Arguments contribute to a culture of war and future conflict. Critical & argumentative people are losers, not because they may be needy or unpopular because they are losing the opportunity to be kind, play, dance, hug, and enjoy life. Every minute they waste attacking you is a lost chance for doing something joyful with their limited time on earth.*

59. Prostitution - Not Ilegal But A Vice Men Should Avoid

The dancer on stage finished her routine and walked off stage, nearly naked. The DJ announced the next girl was coming out on stage. When he asked the audience to give a round of applause to a new dancer, Will's back straightened, and he studied the curtain's movements. Was it her? A busty sexy brunette with athletic long legs emerged in a pink bikini. No, this was not his 'Angel' Thank God.

His woman was sexy enough to work here, but she was far too thoughtful and decent to work in such an unseemly building full of leering adults.

"Why do governments turn away from public stands and allow sex and prostitution right in their back yard? The conflict between the dark and light side causes humans to have both desire and revulsion for the same object. That's why you may see the same politicians that campaign for restrictive laws to get hookers off the street also being arrested in a brothel."

"Ha, ha, ha. That's funny. Many news stories are so compelling to read because we are reading about our foolish hypocrisy." said Will.

"The cultural conflict and hidden religious taboos about sexual desire cause a great deal of anxiety and guilt in the population. Rather than seen as a rational, health act of love and procreation, sex outside of marriage has been driven underground into back alleys & the nighttime where decent folk can pretend it does not exist."

"It's not as bad as it used to be. As long as it's consensual, people don't care who has sex with who", argued Will.

"Well, in your socio-economic group within the United States, that's maybe true. Most of the world is still very conservative about sexual relations. Sure, people have long-term relationships and get married to have 'community sanctioned' sex, but anything outside is frowned on and firmly shamed."

 "Women are especially emotionally unsettled by peer groups if they appear overly sexual. Men feel guilty for having 'aggressive' desires when they glance at and talk to attractive women in bars, clubs, and schools. We learn to feel shameful for having sexual desires when we should be discovering how to understand our emotional needs."

"I see that point of view. I feel a little guilty for being a part of that culture. My high school friends called some sexy girls' sluts' and the cold ones' nice girls'. It's not cool to judge people for desiring what they want," Will said.

"Just your friends?" questioned Morgan. "Inexplicably, people swing between being promiscuous in their sexuality and then rigid and stern about it as a public stance. Some authorities ban the sex trade and then indulge themselves when no one is looking.

"Older, undesirable & married men can only obtain consensual sex from beautiful young women through paying for it with cash, drugs, or other material means. So a natural & beautiful act is commercialized and turned into another commodity that is bartered and sold."

"I am glad there is no prostitution on my street," said Will.

"Don't be so sure of that."

"There are many reasons why honest and nice bystanders allow crime and depravity around them. Citizens don't stop crimes because the wrongdoer is a friend or the victim is not a friend or even an enemy. Passive neighbors may allow it for personal reasons. They believe it's not their problem, or they don't want to become a snitch, or they can't figure out the correct decision going forward.

Will said, "I don't get involved with community issues because it just gives me more unpleasant problems to fret about."

"And that's the seventh reason. Why are we here? This place doesn't seem like your kind of thing."

"Thanks to you, I have the strain of exhaustion. Driving around when everything is closed is boring. This place is less depressing than trying to stay warm in my car."

"Yet you entered this place, an establishment which seems to offer the pleasures of sensuality and then closes the curtain on it, leaving most men completely unsatisfied. But no worries, you are not alone in being drawn into peeking into this lifestyle."

"First, men of a certain age desire what they can no longer have, sex with young, beautiful women. Some feel emasculated by their declining body and their aging partner and want to recapture their youth. Some just like to indulge in the fantasy of sexual attention and respect."

"Then again, younger men can be impulsive and greedy themselves. Some are in stable relationships but have a masochistic need to have multiple partners. Rather than negotiate terms of a loving relationship so they can have intimate relations with a trusted lover, they open their wallet and have intercourse with random women to satisfy their sexual urges."

Will's cheeks started to burn in shame.

"You look embarrassed…. The spouses of johns are extremely upset when their husbands engage in this behavior. What does it say about her skills and value as a romantic partner? Rather than confront the husbands about this illicit behavior, they sweep it under the rug as a form of resentful repression, or they will engage in vicious arguments about money issues, laziness, or some other conflict that flares up."

"And then the prostitutes themselves. A few do it because they have a strong sexual appetite and find the work lucrative. Most would rather not but are trying to feed their illegal drug or shopping addictions and can't earn this kind of money elsewhere. This capitalism of sex can be embarrassing and dehumanizing for both prostitute and john, but they do it regardless."

"Where there are prostitutes who turned to this life to escape another darker past, there are managers who pimp these women, steal and manipulate from them and often beat them and set them into dangerous drug habits."

Will commented. "Depressing stuff, man."

"All these sin industries exist because humans are running around looking for solutions to their inadequacies, building Lifebooks lacking key pages of instruction, and asking random & foolish friends for advice. Had more children received better guidance from their parents and community, they would not reach for senseless band-aid solutions that are ultimately unfulfilling and self-destructive."

Morgan got up from his chair and pulled Will up to his feet. The younger man was feeling woozy; maybe it was the three beers. He followed his hallucination out of the stage area, down the corridor, past the bouncer, and outside. "Hey, wait up. Wait for me."

When Will reached the outside of the building, he saw he was alone. A couple of smokers were standing near the back door watching him. More strippers in winter coats. Not as pretty as the ones inside. Or was it the flashing lights and dark shadows that made them look better than the truth of natural light? More deception. More liars.

Will dropped his car keys in a puddle of muddy snow and uttered a few curse words. Now his hands were wet, cold, and dirty. This inebriated man should not drive, but nobody with integrity was there to block him from getting behind the wheel. Will's BMW disappeared into the night.

RULE OF PRINCIPLE 39: *Sex outside of marriage is not immoral but breaking marriage vows is. Do not feel guilty or shameful for being attracted to other people. Single or married, you will be charmed by potential mates. Be respectful of your relationships & partner's desires.*

It's not strange to have a sex drive; after all, you are human. Understanding cheating might be a both a natural process of biology and a moral failing to honor relationships. Nevertheless, you will have to pay the price for betraying your partner.

60. Night 21 - BREAKUP

Peering through the window, pushing the shade aside, Will stared at the back of Angel's head as she walked away down the sidewalk to her Honda SUV. At least she had the decency to break up with him in person.

He went to the kitchen to find a can of beer as if quenching his thirst would dampen his heart's anger. His ex-girlfriend had used him. Just as he suspected, she was shopping around looking for new relationships before deciding to go back to her current beau.

He touched his cheeks spontaneously and then laughed at himself in embarrassment as he realized he was checking whether tears had fallen from his eyes. There will be no crying today. Will decided he would not give her the satisfaction.

I want you, but I don't want this, she told him. What does that even mean? She did not know. When he said to her that his team was starting on a new project that would consume most of his hours, she lost it.

A former dancer and singer, this expressive and creative woman would be sweet and lovely one moment and set off into a fiery tantrum the next. She was frustrated with her situation, but Angel could not translate her emotions into words. What's wrong? Will would ask her repeatedly while tip-toeing around comments that would set her off again. She did not know.

She accidentally revealed that she wanted a better version of him. The guy he was supposed to become but never reached. Will lost his cool too. Then he realized the blonde was right. Yet, there was no way on God's green earth; he would concede the point.

Opening the window blinds again, he could see Angel was sitting in her car, looking at her phone. She glanced up at his apartment, and Will hastily moved away so she would avoid him watching her.

Breakups are never easy, especially if you had nearly a dozen of them with the same person under the darkness of winter. The pain was still fresh in their memories.

They knew it was better to rip that bandage off quickly in one single motion, yet this couple could not break it off swiftly. Separating a year ago had been a deliberate, tortuous process, as the lovers slowly peeled the wrapping off their wounds, allowing tiny pricks of misery to consume hours of infighting as they untangled their lives from each other.

61. Drug Abuse - Don't Worsen Problems By Insulting Victims

"Have you heard about this war on drugs?" asked Morgan. The apparition was sitting on Will's kitchen counter, drinking a cup of hot black coffee.

"Yes, it is going on for over fifty to a hundred years in the United States. Since it is still going on unabated, I would say that it has been a near-complete failure," said Will.

Morgan took another sip. "Why do you think your dark side makes you break the law with illegal drug use?"

"How did you know whether I have…? Never mind. I don't know. Maybe just to fit in the group? Maybe I felt pressure to say yes to the host. Curiosity? Help me here!" wondered Will.

"You just can't make yourself say it, can you? Your fear and anxiety about whether you are good enough to meet your parents (and society) expectations make you behave in unpredictable ways. Like smoking weed or PCP at a party?"

Will was speechless. "I never thought of myself that way. Does this mean I am crazy?"

"Of course not. You are doing what the mass of humanity does. Some chose to overeat, others drink to excess while underage, and you smoke weed."

"It helps me relax and concentrate."

"If you had more confidence in yourself, you could be completely relaxed and think clearly without the use of any stimulants," said Morgan.

"Can you tell me why the illegal drug trade was such a high priority for law enforcement, at least until the war on terror?" asked Will.

"Governments bans illegal drug usage because excessive consumption causes folks to commit more property theft or damage, and become socially unstable, unreliable employees. The human and financial devastation is of concern to authorities because it costs tremendous tax dollars to house and treat addicts."

"Illegal underground drugs are also a threat to law and order because violent gangs can make vulnerable neighborhoods too dangerous for the police to operate. Businesses, schools, and medical centers find economic activity in gang-controlled areas too weak to sustain themselves.

"Every state in history has failed to prevent the spread of illegal drugs, and usage is so prevalent that criminals smuggle in a constant supply into schools, army bases, and prisons."

"Governments can not admit that they are hopelessly outmanned and outmaneuvered, so they lie about their success. Citizens believe that police departments are seizing huge quantities of drugs at the border and jailing thousands of criminals. In truth, the police and border control can only find a fraction of the smuggled drugs and only serve to cut supply and drive up prices."

"Can you see the hypocrisy here? **Many take illegal drugs to relieve all the anxiety and misery of living in a harsh mechanistic economy that does not care about its citizens. Yet all the prescription drugs to help alleviate stress, anxiety, depression, phobia, sleeplessness, and attention deficits are sold by the very industrial-military complex that is causing many of these illnesses."**

"Instead of helping us cope, pharmacies and medical facilities overmedicate our families and bill us for our troubles. Illegal drug sellers offering similar stimulants like meth, cocaine, and heroin, are arrested and imprisoned while pharma companies get insurance payments and tax subsidies. Of course, drug companies don't shoot up city blocks & break the law, but they are selling the same doped up band-aid solution as the criminals are."

"Really? Aren't you a little stupid about this?" Will disagreed with this.

"You got me! I'm just angry about the whole dang thing. Of course, prosecutors should imprison gang members. But when Purdue Pharma triggered that opioid crisis by convincing doctors to prescribe OxyContin, millions became addicted[cxii]. Two hundred thousand users died from an overdose, and government treatment cost over two trillion dollars."

"Even though the company paid eight billion in fines and went bankrupt, the Sackler family walked away with ten billion dollars. Who is the bigger drug dealer? The man on the street corner or the executive in the office?"

"What if governments legalized and regulated illegal drugs so they could get a piece of the action?" asked Will

"That is highly controversial. Some experts say if authorities lowered prices, addicts would not need to steal or prostitute themselves, and crime would go down. Prisons would have fewer inmates because police would charge fewer people for selling and possession. There would also be less heroin, meth, and opioid deaths if makers used safer ingredients than the crap street dealers manufacturer."

"And then the drug epidemic would get out of control…" said Will.

"That is another lie of the culturescape. The shadow desires what is forbidden. If you take away the illegality of participation, many people lose interest when they cannot rebel against restrictions imposed on them. Some countries that both decriminalized drugs and have established treatment programs have seen falling rates of drug use[cxiii]."

"As I said before, don't trust the authorities when they tell you what to buy or who the real criminals are. Often the food and drug manufacturing companies are spreading outdated propaganda that is false, or worse, dangerous. Think for yourself. Many don't care about your well being."

"As for me, when it comes to psychiatric medicine and treatment, I have been very skeptical about the side effects and the possibilities of long term dependency. If anyone recommends medication for mental issues, I will search for alternative solutions before putting pills in my mouth," said Will.

"Agreed." Morgan nodded his head and got up off the sofa.

RULE OF PRINCIPLE 40 - *Do not verbally abuse or deride people in your care or your family circle. Evil starts like a seed and grows like a weed until it kills the beauty around it. The killing of one's spirit through daily insults is an even greater sin than monetary theft. Yes, you read that right.*

Emotional abuse is worse than stealing because many people break into addictions or other dysfunctions to cope. When people stop working, voting, volunteering, and paying taxes, towns fall apart, crime, drug abuse, gambling, and prostitution soon follow. In the absence of protecting one another, we tend to lean into sinful behaviors.

62. Shoplifting When You Steal, Other Customers Pay

"Have you ever lifted anything from a store?" asked Morgan? He was looking out the window at the retail store mini-mall across the street from Will's apartment building.

"Stealing? No. Never. Not once." he replied vehemently.

"Yes, you were raised to be a good kid. Your parents gave you what you needed, and it rarely appealed to your sensibilities to shoplift merchandise for your enjoyment.

"If it is true that one in eleven people in North America has stolen from stores, that equates to over thirty million shoplifters[cxiv]. And the weird thing is most are not stealing because they can't afford it. They do it for other non-monetary psychological reasons."

"That is too many people. Why do they do it?" Will asked.

"Sometimes, your dark side shows up while you are in a store, and you can't hold back your urges, so you grab something you find irresistible and sneak it out the doors. No, that's a weak explanation."

"Let's try this idea. Many shoplifters have the selfish need to get a thrill of excitement or show off to friends or get things for free, and this compels them to sneak clothes, food, and other merchandise out of the store. This feeling of danger and recklessness can be intoxicating to someone with an average dull life. "

"If other shoppers see them steal, they judge them silently and harshly or look on in approval. Either way, the vast majority say nothing because they believe it is the store owner's dilemma and not their problem. People hate confrontation at all costs, and they also don't like to give bad news to the employees, so they keep their mouths closed. "

"You think that people don't treat this as a serious crime, so it becomes a pastime rather than a degradation of community standards?"

"That is clever, Will."

"Stealing for enjoyment comes from a feeling of lack and insecurity. Even wealthy people shoplift, so it's not about what you own, but how full or empty you perceive your life."

"When we are frightened and worried about threats like joblessness, illness, hurricanes, or going hungry, we become less generous and are more likely to do one of three things: hurting others, hating strangers, or hoarding.[cxv] Shoplifting is an unconscious manifestation of hoarding."

"Taking things that don't belong to us and storing them away gives us temporary relief from our anxieties and worries. There are millions of closets and garages filled to the brim with stuff either stolen or purchased."

"I would have thought these shoplifters sold their pinched items quickly or threw away the evidence. This is unbelievable", said Will

"If you want to know my best theory, many acts of thrill-seeking that harm others are trying to fill a hole created sometime in childhood. Parents nurture love between themselves and their kids until children learn to love themselves unconditionally, without needing other people. Something went wrong in the process."

"Compulsive shoplifters have pervasive negative thoughts that border on pessimistic. They can see all their mistakes or review all signs of disapproval from others and run it through their heads like a horror show. Shoplifting gives temporary relief from our worries."

"And they think 'if my life is this bad, stealing won't make it worse"?" ventured Will.

"No, that is not it at all. Shoplifters don't think about the consequences of their actions or more significant life issues at that moment when they break the law."

"These minor criminals feel that they have been wronged and believe they are making an unfair situation right again.[cxvi] They are taking back control by seizing what was taken from them in the past. This anxiety is a temporary feeling, of course. It can relieve stress temporarily, yet this pervasive sense of lack is a reoccurring mood that shows up at the least convenient times. Compulsive shoplifters feel deep shame and embarrassment but can't stop."

"Is there some therapy or cognitive behavior reframing techniques that work to help them?"

"Some therapy can help, but this is a tough nut to crack. We live in a very permissive society, and there is little to discourage people from quitting. Many shoplifters become very good at stealing and hiding their problems, and they rarely get caught by stores or their families."

"When discovered, stores detain the shoplifters and release them with a warning. Courts don't want to prosecute these low dollar crimes when more serious crimes are pending. Police officers go after big busts and not in arresting petty thieves."

"I get the feeling that you don't view this as a serious problem as other issues we discussed. Did you know businesses add the cost of shoplifting and employee theft to the price tag, so we, the consumer, are paying for it in the end?"

"It puts millions of store employees on edge because they view all customers with suspicious eyes until they see the customer reach the cash register. All forms of dishonest, theft, and vandalism disrupt the natural flow of trust and compassion we have for each other. If you think it does not affect you, you are wrong."

"Shoplifters are stealing from other shoppers because managers increase retail prices to cover losses. In short, dishonest players are stealing from you and not the institutions that you think are taking the losses."

"The idea of confronting thieves in the act of ratting on them makes me feel nauseous. What else can we do?"

"Vigilante justice is not the wisest course of action. How about speaking your mind about problems in the community? Be supportive of those who are struggling with addictions. Voice your disapproval on behaviors that many seem to think are fine but betray the neighborhood trust. It's time to end the silence on declining moral values."

"Ahhhh. If there are no more questions, I will call it a night."

"Okay, that's fine! Leave me here with all these nasty thoughts in my head. You know I haven't slept in weeks."

Morgan got off the kitchen counter, adjusted his tie, and straightened out his pants: "As I recall, you have some good books in your closet unfinished. Reading might help. Later, Will."

"Bye, Mike, err Morgan," Will said his farewell.

RULE OF PRINCIPLE 41: *Unless you are Robin Hood, please don't pocket things that don't belong to you. It is immoral to shoplift from stores and steal gadgets from businesses, schools, and governments, but many thieves can't see the bigger picture.*

Few shoplifters would steal from their Nana or beloved friend but would like to payback rich and powerful organizations by retrieving ill gotten gains. Shocker! All institutions know how to transfer the cost of theft to other customers and taxpayers. When you steal, someone else's grandmother is paying for your indiscretion.

63. Night 22 - INTERRUPTION

The phone rang in the midnight hour, stirring Will from a comatose state of mind. He still could not get that sweet sleep he craved, and yet even this rude interruption of his tossing and turning sent him into a rage.

"Hello?" he said gruffly into the receiver. "Who is this?"

The sound of deep breathing filled his ear. It was unmistakably male in tone, and Will would have guessed that the caller was a heavy-set adult from the labored breathing.

The caller paused as if about to say something, and Will's annoyance at this invasion of his privacy grew. Will was just about to hang up when he heard a new sound.

A single expletive word flew out of the phone and slapped him in the face. The call ended with a thump as if the aggressor had slammed down the receiver of a corded push-button home phone.

The victim of this strange prank stared at his phone in amazement. Could this have been a wrong number? A practical joke? No, the caller wanted to bash him verbally but bailed out at the last minute.

Will's eyes started to close again. He rocked backward onto his bed. Twenty minutes later, he was wide awake anew. Will pulled his coat off the hanger and headed outside.

64. Corporate Ethics - Please Don't Copy Sociopathic Behaviors

Will was slow in his stride; his legs were feeling sore after spending many restless nights. All he could get was a few minutes of sleep here and a few minutes there. Morgan was matching his pace as they left his building. He was glad to have some company. Any intelligent conversation was better than being alone with his thoughts.

"Have you heard the expression, a few bad apples spoil the whole bunch?"

"Yes, older people say that all the time," replied Will.

"True, Many conservatives & politicians have changed the saying to 'it's only a few bad apples.' Meaning that if there is corruption in the police force, politics, medical professionals, teachers, or anyone in authority, there are only a handful of people breaking the rules.[cxvii]"

"They are implying that everyone else in the organization is honest, decent, and incorruptible. Such deceit justifies blaming an individual or two for systematic decay and allowing the rest to continue as usual with their everyday hypocrisy."

"And you are saying that is not true?" asked Will

"Like rot, depravity can grow until all, but the incorruptible is tainted. **When stealing seems safe and profitable, many**

feel the temptation to copy the perpetrators. If lying and exaggerating is seen as a key characteristic of the wealthy and powerful, it becomes the standard practice of day to day conversation. A few bad apples can spoil the bunch!"

"A fascinating documentary came out with the premise that corporations are constructed and designed to act like sociopathic personalities. A sociopath is an ambitious antisocial being with no understanding or empathy for the hurt feelings caused by its immoral, bad behavior."

"Corporations are similar to sociopaths because their primary directive is to produce profits even if they harm the people, communities, and the environment around them.[cxviii] The difference is that corporate culture infects the rest of society, while individuals mainly harm those around them."

"Corporate sociopathic behavior spreads to other organizations?" asked Will.

"Yes, when they dominate the economy, people inside and out the corporation must obey their commands or suffer the consequences. They can do whatever is legally permissible, move to other nations, be bought up, sold, merged, and made insolvent as is necessary.

"This means that a corporation can and will act immorally to make profits with no loss of wealth or reputation to its shareholders. The shareholders can legitimately claim they are unaware of unethical practices because they do not manage the firm, the executives do."

"How is this possible if governments can regulate big businesses?... Never mind. You already talked about political corruption and campaign finance problems," Will said.

"So you were listening. Humans are ingenious at taking the worst of their impulses and outsourcing their criminality to other objects or people."

"The accused can claim: 'It was not me! Whiskey and Gin made me crash that car' or 'I did not hire those workers who died in that factory fire. It was that other supplier who was responsible.' The besieged can say, 'I am not responsible' and 'You can't blame me for that," and such tactics often succeed."

Will responded, "Investors can act immorally and harm other consumers without having any feelings of guilt by having their investments in corporations do it for them in the pursuit of profits. I see that now."

"All of these are subconscious actions, of course. People don't want to harm others (unless they are mentally sick), but we are motivated by many things in life that overwhelm our attention. We don't see that our profits and dividends come at the cost of punishing externalities."

Will asked, "Externalities?"

"That means unintended negative effects of doing business. Corporations can layoff workers, sell defective products, or cause pollution. Those externalities are not the financial responsibility of the business because shareholders usually don't have to pay for it.

"When you create a business structure owned by hundreds or thousands of people, and none of them are personally responsible for the losses or damages caused by that corporation, you have to rely on the management of the business to act responsibly. Executives are under tremendous pressure to produce profits for shareholders to the exclusion of all else. They are not going to fight the system either."

"Government regulation on corporations has crumbled over the last thirty years, and these businesses are racing all around the world to exploit oil, wheat, gas, corn, sugar, and metal resources as fast as they can."

"Workers and cities compete for corporations' favor to establish factories and offices to create jobs and tax revenue. The lowest-paid countries with the least amount of worker protection and environmental oversight often win this race to the bottom."

"But evil, theft, and dishonesty pre-date these corporate organisms by thousands of years." protested Will.

"Yes, of course, some businessmen have always been competitive and ruthless, but never at this scale. Unethical behavior has spread from sociopathic corporations to the rest of society because they control most of the world economy. Corporations are a new way of transforming unbridled power into an army of cash-generating machines that weld constructive and destructive forces that no community or government can stop."

Will said, "You are exaggerating."

"Am I? Witness all the political influences by companies with budgets as large as the government they are pressuring. See profitable factories closed and towns ground down of the economic force that sustained them. Look at how forests, mountains, and fish stocks are being decimated without arrest because property rights allow it. Governments no longer run the world; sociopathic corporations do."

"And there is nothing we can do about it?" Will asked.

"If you don't like the conversation, change it. Start your own culture. Build a business the way you like it. Copy what corporations do well but run it at a higher standard of ethics than they operate at."

The two men paused at a street bench. Despite the icy temperature and damp wood, Will sat down to rest his legs. They had been walking down past a series of storefronts that appeared as old and tired as Will felt. The young man slowly got up with the grace and demeanor of someone twice his age, and they continued down the street.

RULE OF PRINCIPLE 42: *Sociopathic corporations are causing misery for countless citizens, but demand workers to pretend nothing is amiss. Far too many people feel they should never display anger, feel sad, or have envious thoughts - if they could only learn to be happy, cheerful, and pleasant all the time. This cultural teaching may cause mental illness and increase unethical behavior as keeping appearances becomes paramount to internal codes of conduct.*

This insanity is not only unrealistic; it is unhealthy as well. You should feel sad when people leave you or die. You are supposed to feel competitive when rivals earn more. It is healthy to be angry when people break essential rules meant to protect you. Don't apologize for being a caring person when cynicism is the order of the day.

65. Therapy - Take Charge Of Your Life; Others Will Screw It Up

As they ambled along the sidewalk, Morgan changed the topic again:

"If you are even a little aware of societal changes, you might have seen news reports about the rise in drug use, obesity, depression, anxiety, sexual abuse, stress, and attention deficit disorder. Why is that?"

"Life is getting tougher?" Will guessed.

"There are strong arguments for that stance. Still, there has never been a more prosperous time in history. Have you considered the idea that many residents are lost and confused, wandering around looking for someone to give them, these disoriented souls, some direction for their lives?"

Morgan continued, "Could it be that sacrificing one's life for popularity, wealth, and status symbols provoke one to abandon reason & harm their sense of integrity?"

"Put another way, using dishonesty, cheating, manipulation, and abusive language as tactics to get what they want; people fall into mental despair when the realization strikes them. They are both failing at their objectives and turning into a person others despise."

"When the dark side takes over, people shut down emotionally. All energy focuses on the crisis of self, and everything around them becomes a life and death significance. The lack of trust in others causes them to be cautious and halting in their discussions, which is why many conversations are so damn boring and mundane.[cxix]"

"For therapy clients with serious phobias, mental disorders, and malicious tendencies stemming from childhood, the ongoing discussion of past traumas may not help as much as they desire."

"The dark side of both the therapist and patient co-create a dramatic retelling of memories that make negative thoughts feel more real over time and gain a life of their own. The doctor's own shadow compels the curiosity in him or her to get to the bottom of the issue."

"I am confused. Aren't we talking about dishonesty, exploitation, and criminality?" Will asked.

"Eager to fuel your dark side?" chided Morgan. "Of course, the therapists may have the right answers, but clients might refuse to do the work. Some patients come and pay for therapy but do not try to change themselves, fail to do the homework or exercises, and blame their partner, children, boss, parents, friends, anyone else instead of taking personal responsibility for their part in this."

"They want the attention of the therapist, or they like playing the victim, or they are deflecting criticism by showing they are attempting reform. But you want to know if therapy can help hardcore cases like career criminals or mentally disturbed patients?"

"Yeah, I wanna know," Will replied.

"There are rarely easy solutions for chronic problems! Far too many people think that a little prescription medication will make their problem go away. If that does not work, they think a few sessions of mental therapy treatment will work. Nope, not true."

"Ceaseless worrying by an adult about potential threats is very difficult to undo instantly because tens of thousands of repetitive thoughts over time, hardwire it into the brain. So are thoughts of criminality, anger, anxiety, and depression."

"Talking about problems rarely fixes them alone. You have to change to confront the underlying patterns of thought that cause distress. Breaking addictions, erasing racist beliefs, and controlling one's temper will be a deeply emotionally painful struggle because it's a battle of wills between the subconscious and conscious."

Will asked, "But, you don't think the psychologist can help?"

"Of course they can. Counselors & doctors can give coaching, therapy, or provide information. It's mainly a supportive role. The patient himself will have to do the difficult work of ridding himself of this dark cloud of energy.

He might stretch so far as to a complete lifestyle change, including new friends, hobbies, and jobs."

"Our dark side hates change and will fight any identity shift, so it will self-sabotage attempts to go straight. It will subconsciously motivate patients to visit friends who also have criminal leanings or addictions, and these friends will bring them back into the shadows[cxx]."

"It seems like a massive struggle to straighten out our problems," Will said.

"As difficult as learning to walk again. You are fighting a torrent of temptations and opportunities to mess up your life again. Alcoholics Anonymous (AA) have a twelve-step program that works to battle alcoholism. Virtually any destructive behavior can be removed by following a simple twelve-step program, but many compulsive behaviors lack addiction recovery programs. If it takes a village to raise a child, it may take a crowd to liberate an addicted grown-up."

"So it's much easier to treat unwelcome behavior in childhood than later in life. As you said before, if the parents did a better job raising their children, some criminals and addicts would enjoy a more satisfying adulthood," Will stated.

"Kind of a simplistic way of seeing it, but yeah, you are stating the truth," replied Morgan

The companions had circled the area crossing five different streets, and returned to Will's apartment building. Will shivered as if shards of ice had penetrated his garments. He trembled after he remembered that he had just spent forty minutes having a conversation with a hallucination.

The man, Morgan, walking away from him, was still a figment of his imagination, and he needed to climb out of this abyss of insomnia and back into normality.

RULE OF PRINCIPLE 43: *You are in charge of your decisions. Take responsibility for your actions. Don't blame or ask others to pay the price of your bad decisions. An adult takes charge while a child will ask for rescue. When you defer leadership to others, they get some of the rewards, and you suffer most of the consequences*

66. Night 23 - QUESTIONS

Will trudged into his lonely apartment after work. Was this his entire life? Was this all there is? As he leaned his hand against the kitchen counter to pull off his winter boots, a bit of color grabbed his eye. The African Violet plant his mother gave him was sprouting up tiny flower petals. These slivers of purple and blue signified new vitality in this potted plant. Was this a harbinger of something good yet to come?

Angel's call surprised him. As he recognized her voice, she blurted out an apology, and he did so in return. The phone call was filled with long pauses as if the emotional connotations of each word said raised the stakes of this frayed connection.

Where was the old Will with whom she had a love affair? He was there but not there. Will felt heartened that she was still talking and grousing about their relationship. When it came to having fun, Angel was never at a loss for options, so he surmised she sought the sweet agony of partnership over choosing more hedonistic pleasures.

Will confessed to his love that not only he could not sleep; he was having dreams filled with immorality and wickedness. The hallucinations, those stories she would not understand. His energy & enthusiasm were draining to dangerous levels, and he was hanging on by a thread. He desperately wanted to give her all of himself but just was not able to rejuvenate this vitality to normality.

She did not know what to say. Too many men had enraptured her with their words but failed to live up to expectations. Men were so good at talking about what they could be but not at being who they were. He replied he would change jobs and put her first, above all else, just for the chance at happiness.

That was not good enough. Angel did not want a man who could give her the world and lacked the energy to enjoy it with her. The blonde wanted someone who had the same enthusiasm for life in his fifties, seventies, and nineties as those kids who were so excited to get into college or purchase their first starter car.

Will confessed he did not know how to be that person except when he was with her. His mind was racing & muddled. He could not think anymore. Could she let him wrestle with the idea of who he should be? Please give him a few days, he begged.

Angel replied that she was as confused as he was. Please give her something. Something she could work with so she could have assurance her time was not going to waste. She said her goodbyes.

Will told her he did not want to hang up on her. He was not ready to say farewell. They reminisce for another twenty minutes about their best & earliest dates, and then she snuck a quick bye before hanging up.

67. Terrorists - Promote Good Behavior To Interested Parties

Back in the apartment, Will was having trouble following Morgan's thoughts. He was both confused about the state of his relationship with Angel and how he would get back to normalcy.

"When young children experience such dark trauma such as the violent death of a parent or a brutal rape and assault, their dark side can completely take over and sees the world as only a violent and dark place[cxxi]. Add racism and xenophobia, and you have one deadly cocktail of hate. Some terrorists are willing to harm others and themselves because their delusional reasoning sees it as righting a wrong."

"Most people are terrible at understanding why they perform cruel acts and stop themselves from asking what their values are. Whatever is inside you, whether good or evil, wants to grow and spread. The dark side of a terrorist leader desires to recruit the impoverished and vulnerable to spread the fear and anxiety that matches his worldview."

"Terrorists willfully cause pain and suffering among millions of news viewers by creating a dramatic and scary spectacle that feels more dangerous than is the reality."

"I read in a book that terrorist groups have limited numbers of bombs and assassins, so they use drama and theatrics to showcase attacks as bolder, more random and traumatic than its actual impact. That's why they go after church gatherings, stadiums, and cafes full of people," confirmed Will.

"Smart boy. **All humanity's collective shadow suffers because we recognize the terrorist attack as a personal threat to our existence. The dark side in us receives more confirmation bias that outsiders are untrustworthy, and we put up more barriers to love and respect each other.**

"Many organizations will use this fear to advance their agenda. The news media uses terrorism to get more viewers, and terrorists use journalists to broadcast their messages. Politicians seize the momentum to fund anti-terrorism campaigns that help them maintain power. Racists use it to confirm their biases and hatred of minorities."

Will checked the conversation. "Hold it right there. Ninety-nine point nine percent of violence and war victims choose not to join terrorist organizations and blow themselves up. What is the cause of all this?"

"It's the suppression of the spirit of being human. These children lack essential love and have little hope for a brighter future. Whether their parents were cruel, neglectful, or disappeared, the boy who grows up to be a terrorist did not receive enough love to neutralize the hurt he felt from his loss. He did not learn how to ask for, accept, and give loving interactions in a healthy relationship.[cxxii] A child who grew up full of love has little room to give out hate."

"Are you asking us to give sympathy? I can't do that." Will stated. "What about that hope thing?"

"You have every right to hate terrorists because they are among the vilest and disgusting creatures on earth. And the most misguided."

"Terrorists have so many negative feelings that they can't see the good in humanity. They have lost hope in the future. Some are mentally ill, many are unemployed, almost all live in poverty, and most lack romantic relationships[cxxiii]. Yet some are also well educated & do have family support in what they are doing. It takes all kinds. These boys or men are susceptible to the evil influences of those masterminds who prey on hopelessness and despair."

"Once these ignorant killers are welcomed and indoctrinated into their cultish families, their values of what is right and wrong is twisted and turned upside down. Out of loyalty and dedication to the cause, the terrorist comes to believe that murder and suicide is the right and honorable thing to do. Many will grab onto false hope, even if they must die to believe in it."

"That's pretty sick. Can we talk about something else?" asked Will.

RULE OF PRINCIPLE 44: *Teach how to develop a high character to worthy students. We need more teachers of ethics, principles, and morality because society ignores good behavior in favor of allowing destructive forms of materialism, hedonism, and workaholism. Demonstrate your goodness freely and without embarrassment. The world needs to see acts of kindness and generosity to counteract a common belief that the world is turning rotten.*

68. Gig Economy - Offering & Accepting Poor Pay Is Often Immoral

"Okay, what's next? Serial Killers? Hitler? Aliens from outer space? What is it?" Will asked. He adjusted the pillows behind his back as he tried to focus on his guest.

"Mocking questions from a conflicted mind that still fails to grasp the gold in suffering wisdom and knowledge. The Gig Economy."

"Really?" Will pulled his leather ottoman towards his black recliner.

"The dark side of man co-ops good intentions and turns well-meaning desires into deceit, harm, and anger. The emotional conflict between established taxi companies and ride-sharing apps like Uber and Lyft is another example when the industry chooses to exploit others for profit and gain."

"Taxi drivers have always had a tough job driving in heavy traffic going from fare to fare. At least if they worked forty to sixty hours, they could earn enough to provide for their families. Silicon Valley software companies Lyft and Uber have made ride-sharing much easier and prevalent. Users say they can get more reliable pick up times and cleaner cars than taxis, which can be hard to find at certain times."

"I like using Uber & Lyft. It's easy, convenient, and cheap." declared Will.

"Yeah, that's the problem. Cheap. Contractual driving jobs are pay per fare gig economy jobs. The income can be substantial if there is a high demand for customers and a low supply of drivers. Instead, drivers with a car who needs a side income to survive have flooded the market, causing an oversupply of rideshare cars."

"Unfortunately, this competition between Taxis and Uber drivers has driven down fare prices and made it much more difficult to make a living from driving."

"Many drivers don't have a choice. They can't find work elsewhere." protested Will.

"And many drivers do have full-time jobs & college education. Yet they willingly do work that is below their capabilities. If one gig job fails, they fail to learn and repeat past mistakes by moving to another substandard job."

"The ride-sharing and food delivery app companies misrepresent the daily revenue and expenses of joining. They tell their new hires all about the revenue earned but do not explain that gas, insurance, and car wear and tear eat into earnings so much that the average hourly earnings can fall below minimum wage levels.[cxxiv] Many drivers don't realize this, so they can drive for months before they realize they would earn more money doing almost anything else."

"The younger generation recognizes the unequal balance of power in the employee-corporate relationship, and many have chosen self-employment as an alternative to nine-five corporate-think. However, **these entrepreneurs lack the wisdom to choose the right venture and select gig app work, agency sales, or network marketing that leaves them just as chronically broke and restless as the underemployed."**

"So all the passengers should give their drivers a larger tip to make up the difference?" ventured Will

"That can help a little. The point is those good intentions to provide an alternative way of getting around or delivering food may have hurt as many people as it helped. The app companies' greed and fear to return profits to the venture capitalists caused them to accept too many drivers. They also raised their commission rates so that drivers have moved from a satisfactory hourly rate to one that is less than minimum wage."

"Great, you just trashed another industry. Isn't anyone honest these days?" complained Will

"Will, as I said before, all industries are made up of human workers. The temptation to cheat and get ahead is too great for some. They will cut unfair deals and exploit the weaknesses of others."

"Let's call it, this game, on account of rain," Morgan joked.

"That joke makes no sense. We are indoors." Will shot down the corny pun. "But before you go, can I share my theory with you?"

"Yeah, sure, Will."

"When you run out of things to tell me, will my mind drill you out of existence as unnecessary? No more sleepless nights once the lessons are over?" asked Will.

"Maybe, maybe not."

RULE OF PRINCIPLE 45: *Don't rip employees off. Pay fair wages and write contracts that benefit both parties, even if you have the upper hand. Bad deals create more conflict, lawsuits, and employee turnover than businesses desire. Is winning worth the stress and heartache from breaking the spirit of people? If you are an average negotiator at deal-making (and you are!), you probably are losing as much as you are winning.*

69. Night 24 - BRILLIANCE

It was incredible. Out of Will's muddled & tired mind popped up a point of inspiration. He had a brilliant idea while driving home from work, so the engineer texted her right away.

He asked her a question. Would she agree to spend all their free time searching to discover her real passion? Once they found her 'joie de vivre,' they could build her a dream job or business, and he would work his career around her?

Angel messaged him back. That idea was sweet, but she did not want to be anyone's fantasy. Camping out and building a castle around her should not be the sole purpose of a man's life. That would make her feel like a burden, and she could not live with herself if her partner gave up everything he wanted just to try to make her happy.

Inspired by her passion for acts of kindness, he shared an alternative idea. He had expressed a few times to his ex-wife, but she did not seem enthusiastic about it.

Will knew of an employer that would allow him to take a month off each year for vacation. While in high school, he dreamed of flying off to Africa or India and volunteering to build new schools and hospitals. Civil engineers were in great demand, and Will was very optimistic that sponsors would pay for the building materials he needed. They could travel together, but if she could not come, they had a backup plan. The couple would separate for twenty-eight days &

nights, and he would give her a night to remember on his return.

What a great idea, Angel exclaimed. She loved it. But she only had two weeks vacation? No problem. They could coordinate traveling together, and she could fly home ahead of him. They could spend time together overseas, making a difference, and still have a romantic rendezvous on his return.

Make it happen, she said. Show me you are serious by actually doing the work. She told Will she wanted this relationship to move from 'a maybe' to a definite yes as much as he did.

70. Lawyers - Choose Your Profession Wisely To Be Who You Want To Be

Will was watching some unusual sports league in a foreign land on a channel he rarely clicked on. He could not make heads or tails of this weird rough game called rugby.

Morgan materialized on the sofa next to him. "Hi, Will."

"Hi. I hate it when you do that. Can you knock first? Or at least emerge from another room?" he complained.

"Sorry about that. I can't control your mind. You cause me to appear in the way your subconscious mind desires. Sorry."

"It's all so confusing how you have come into my life," Will stated.

"Who is the most hated group of people in America?" asked Morgan, ignoring Will's state of confusion.

"Well, it's a close tie between lawyers and politicians, but since we already covered politicians, it has to be the legal profession," answered Will.

Glaring at him for getting it right, Morgan began: "Lawyers are hated and feared because they are considered greedy, expensive, and somewhat unreliable, yet necessary. This dislike is justified because lawyers, more than anyone, are responsible for shielding the assets of the corporate elite and preventing substantial transformation to the global economy.

"Wherever there are crimes, bribery, kickbacks, pollution, worker exploitation, and other kinds of immorality, lawyers are completing the paperwork and taking their cut."

"The legal industry draws in very competitive, aggressive, and money-driven people. This environment can be toxic for many lawyers who turn to alcoholism, shopping sprees, medication, therapy, and even more workaholism to cope."

"Hey, I have a couple of friends who work as attorneys. They complain the work is incredibly stressful and the hours brutal," Will contributed.

"And those are the lucky ones. Tens of thousands of law graduates pass the bar, desiring to join elite firms who service the wealthy, but these firms only draw in the top law students with prime assignments and lofty salaries. In reality, most average law associates never see a courtroom, earn mediocre salaries, and live in a cubicle for twelve-hour days poring over legal documents."

"So it is a tough business. What is so bad about it?" Will asked.

"The law is about war. Instead of soldiers and tanks, corporations and nations use lawyers and documents. The paranoid, perfectionist, and aggressive personality types do well working here.[cxxv]"

"Lawyers are similar to mercenary foot soldiers for the actual corporate/political structure, and they must keep outsiders from stealing or weakening their power base."

"Either your firm is on the attack or the defense. Having a pessimistic outlook that the worst going to happen is an asset for success. Some lawyers thrive on conflict and winning while others join to attain material success. All these poisonous attitudes spread into other industries outside the law because we can't help adopt behaviors of the most aggressive and successful members."

"I never heard anyone describe the law that way before. The United States has seventy percent of the world's lawyers, with only five percent of the population. Why does it draw so many in?" asked Will.

"The value, prestige, income, and glamour of the profession have led many bright students into this esteemed profession. The reality is that law schools desiring growth and profits accepted far too many students, creating a glut of professionals with law degrees, many who leave the industry quickly after graduation."

"Many students find law school very soul-crushing and competitive as the culture of greed, winning and materialism overwhelms idealistic scholars who aspire to serve the public good."

"The workload, conflict, status-seeking, bullying, and peer pressure all make a sizable portion of lawyers feel

very unhappy. Instead of seeing depression as a signal that it is time to make changes, the suffering lawyer's dark side desires alcohol, medication, and gambling to cope.[cxxvi] Some coping mechanisms turn into a deadly addiction."

"So lawyers, in general, are not as lucky, successful, and happy as the public thinks they are?" asked Will.

"I believe you are asking a question about winning a pyrrhic victory. Is all that money earned worth the energy required to survive such a career?"

"The dark side of each lawyer copes differently under this pressure. Many partners get angry and gossip against or insult the associates who don't thrive in this environment. They can't see their behavior as malicious, so they blame unpopular employees for having character flaws rather than the toxic culture they created."

"From this and other constituents, the legal profession suffers from very high rates of mental disorders. Depression is ubiquitous here and is often a sign that something is wrong[cxxvii]. The sufferer must make new life choices or choose to continue down the same paths."

"The judgment of the shadow lies heavily on the conscience of the depressed lawyer, and many can't admit they made a mistake, so they continue on this false choice at the sacrifice of the best decades of their lives."

"Many, if not all, families of discouraged workaholic lawyers pressure them to remain put in this career. Why would a lawyer quit a prestigious firm to change professions or work solo? Why give up that salary? How will the associate cover his or her debt? A lack of encouragement prevents many from seeking alternative careers."

"Depression means evolution and change, not decline and failure?" Will clarified.

"Yes, it's a way for the subconscious mind to force humans to break away from unhealthy patterns. Some realize it's time to change, but most are either unwilling or unable to suffer through the pain of giving up the known and cling to familiar behavior patterns.[cxxviii] They fail to renegotiate with life and lose the opportunity for rebirth."

"Maybe we should be more compassionate to professionals who seem successful on the outside but are feeling conflict and regret within?" stated Will.

"Let's not slam just the lawyers. Missteps apply to all careers and entrepreneurial ventures. If you are not happy with your job and can't find a company that gives the support you need, that profession may be a poor match for your passions, interests, and personality type. "

"Too many people guess what career they should start because they viewed some impressive television shows or films. Some had a few conversations with the wrong people who have biased & uniformed advice. With little to no research, they invest decades into building a career that was completely wrong for them."

"This reminds me of thought. Trying to achieve your desires without a moral compass is like shoving other shoppers as you race to grab that last sale item you desperately crave. You might get punched or trampled yourself and get nowhere close to the object of your desire. If you beat out the competition, you might have a bitter taste in your mouth as you look back at all the bodies you stepped on."

Morgan walked into the kitchen, disappearing from view. After five minutes, Will got up to see if Morgan was still there. Empty. God damn it. That was very unsettling; why couldn't his esteemed guest have better manners and say goodbye?

RULE OF PRINCIPLE 46: *Please be Ethical. On your deathbed, your respected name matters as much as your success. Morality and ethics can be as important as becoming wealthy and possessing things. Don't mature into a person you regret becoming. What we focus on is what expands. Make room in your life to volunteer, be kind, praise humanity, share, and appreciate others. Notice these are actions and not just thoughts. It would be best if you did some good to be good.*

71. Night 25 - FIRE

Will had a vivid dream that made no sense to him. He was skipping all over the apartment in the dark and messing about like he was three years old again. Thousands of lights danced in front of his eyes. They floated and flew around the rooms like a million dandelion seeds. He reached out to grab a handful, but they all escaped his clutching fingers.

A loud voice called out, and suddenly, all the floating seeds caught on fire like fireworks igniting. The flames leaped onto the walls; the entire room engulfed in fire. Will pounded the melting walls with his fists to escape certain death. A dark void tore open, the wallpaper, drywall & brick crumbled into the pitch-black hole, and he fell into nothingness.

72. Tobacco & Alcohol - Realize Addiction Is Not A Choice

The civil engineer turned on the light in his apartment and found his teacher sitting in the dark kitchen. Will felt his heart pounding in his chest and falling back into its natural rhythms as he realized he was not in danger.

"Okay, Morgan. Why do you keep shocking me like that?"

"I don't know. I believe you see me when you need me. We have just two more lessons to go."

"Really?" Will felt relief.

Morgan dove right in. "Now the executives who run and own tobacco and alcohol businesses, those bastards are truly Machiavellian in every sense of the world. These cunning, scheming, and unscrupulous managers know their products are harming their customers, but continue to sell them regardless."

"By tapping into the need to rebel, relax and have fun, advertisers create a false image of parties and friendship that is very appealing to young consumers searching for meaning and pleasure in their lives."

"Remember, not all addiction is the same. Consumers can drink and smoke just a little without any major disruption to their health and happiness. Others dive deep into the bottle and pack of smokes because they can temporarily forget who they are and what they have become.[cxxix]"

"The most conflicted people in the world, the artists, the outsiders, the rebels, and the non-conformists are most likely to choose the most destructive coping methods, like drinking, to survive in a hostile environment."

Will found himself yawning many times. He could not remember ever being so tired as he was this night. Still, he sat there passively and listened quietly.

"Our dark side will do anything to avoid the truth. It will cause its human host to blame, destroy, shout, and scream at anything that threatens to unmask all the hurt and pain endured.[cxxx] The mind will become disorganized itself so that it will create tasks of manic enthusiasm, conflicted relationships, and unpredictable behavior to keep everyone at bay."

"Late in life, five, ten, twenty years down the road, all these buyers have are bad habits that make them feel deflated and out of control. The joy and pleasure have declined with use now that their internal organs are soaked and familiar with the effects. It takes more drinks than ever to numb the pain. Addicts are likely to contend with heart disease and cancer as their internal organs can no longer take the abuse. That's if they live long enough."

"Users of alcohol, drugs, and tobacco can conclude that there is something seriously wrong with them. After all, most people are not addicted, and many hide it from the public eye much better than they can. Addicts often cannot see the beauty in their own lives because their drug of choice is like a demon on their tail that won't stop tempting them."

"Everyone who can see what is going on loses their patience and compassion for this poor soul. The broken promises, emotional debris, hurt feelings, and unfulfilled potential is too difficult to endure anymore."

"We can only feel hostile, angry, and a sense of hopelessness as we see this victim crawl towards his or her next hit of pleasure. It's not right. They let us down. This failing of moral character is an unjust act towards the construction of the person they could be[cxxxi]."

"We don't see the evil in the manufacturers of our discontent. We think they just make stuff. It does not even enter our minds that the marketers of diversions manipulated their customers into addiction."

"The investors and supporters can rationalize that these products create jobs and fulfill consumer demand, but that does not excuse the negative externalities of addiction, poor health, depression, and every other problem that they cause. "

"The tobacco and alcohol industries are a reflection of what is going in our consciousness. We see the dark side in us, become frightened, and flee away in the other direction. Had we stayed to examine our lives, we would have seen the power and fury in the blackness are allies that can bring about a brighter future.[cxxxii]"

Morgan paused and stood up from the kitchen table.

"Sucking down drugs and indulging in alcohol is like wearing sunglasses. They may temporarily protect our sanity from the glaring shine of our potential, but they also darken the world and prevent us from seeing clearly."

"The steep price to pay is authenticity, honesty, and love because alcohol and drugs are ways you betray yourself from reaching your full potential."

RULE OF PRINCIPLE 47: *If you are not addicted, that's luck & wisdom, not a form of superiority. Some of us are stronger of will than others and that is a gift of the fates. Pity the addicted because it's in our nature to hide from pain. Almost everyone is addicted to something, so don't be rude if your addiction (work, sugar, social media, coffee, worry) is more socially acceptable than those you condemn for universal moral weakness (gambling, stealing, porn, alcohol, drugs).*

73. Social Media - Cut That Sh*t Out Or Suffer FOMO, Trolls, & Envious Anxiety

Will realized Morgan wanted to continue the conversation in the living room. He got up from the kitchen table, shuffled over to his sofa, and lay down as if sitting up was too exhausting to manage. Morgan sat down in the adjoining recliner and continued with his final instruction.

"As we have discussed, humans are capable of behaving very poorly to others. The invention of social media like Twitter, Facebook, and Instagram is like adding rocket fuel to the multi-generational behavior of envy, jealousy, hostility, anger, and fear of others."

"Some leaders think it's just a harmless pastime. They are flat out wrong. Social media in virtual reality will be the main tent pole of our civilization for decades to come and will orient our trajectory towards either growth or chaos."

"The dark side's exposure to social media triggers a backlash of impulsive responses and misunderstandings that turns friends into adversaries, family into enemies, and political parties to cult-like mobs. Is the falsity of social media worth the benefits of establishing and making friends around the world? Time will tell."

"Why is this? Influencers combine words and images to communicate in ways that translate in hundreds of ways."

"Photoshopped, curated fake images signify higher social, physical, and economic status than the person posting has to millions of people. Enormous audiences with various political, cultural, and religious beliefs perceive this in ways that are very unpredictable and combustible."

"In a fast scrolling world where users receive hundreds of blurred posts a day, negative misinterpretations happen every day. Someone could write about spending the day at church, and some in their audience could see that as displaying moral superiority when the writer just ached to share her day's events with friends."

"As we discussed, the images on social media are not accurate portrayals of real life. Influencers will take dozens of photos of a minute event within a twenty-four hour day and post the very best picture. Tens of thousands of attractive images and interesting stories that appeal to the masses rise to the top of the search results. They go viral or trend upwards, and social media users start to believe those popular images reflect authentic normality rather than irregular idealism.[cxxxiii]"

"The users of social media see image after image of the most popular influencers (and their friends) and conclude their personal life and circumstances are inferior and unsatisfactory."

"Whatever you believe in or like, you will encounter others online who disagree with you on your choices. There are millions of people who follow the same stories, articles, and videos as you."

Will yawned again. He stretched out his arms as if that might re-energize him.

"Still, their cultural values and beliefs are very different, and they are not afraid to share their differences in opinion with you. Comments by cruel, hurtful, and immature social media users (trolls) can trigger a harsh and defensive posture from even the most compassionate and kind people[cxxxiv]."

"Facebook, Instagram, and other places on the internet can be joyful places where you share a laugh or get some inspiration. Some will even help you with your most difficult problems. **But they can also make you feel something is wrong with you. The dark feelings of hopelessness, hostility, and anger may replace the lightness of happiness and peace, should you be exposed to the wrong ideas**

"Looking in on envy at the gorgeous partners, homes, and cars that others have that you do not, you might reach for some more chips and cake to soothe your anxiety. Maybe pot or alcohol or something else might numb the pain?"

"Maybe you get inspired to build a better life for yourself. After all, if they can do it, so can you!" You ignore those friends who are drifting away and engage in many business ventures to create your dream life. But your mind desires many things all at once. You start and stop countless plans, unfinished books, and business ideas that all collapse under inertia's weight."

"The notifications of media, emails, phones, and texts all distract you throughout the day, and you find yourself unable to focus. It takes you three hours to do something that should take half an hour because you get caught up in the drama of other peoples' offers and lives. You are no longer yourself but a mirror image of the screen you stare at all day. A personality split into a thousand pieces that are desperately trying to fit in & look cool. "

"In general, the younger you are, the more integral social media is to your life. Young people thirty and under have made social media indispensable to their lives. Except for those who hate it, students and twenty-somethings are on social media hundreds of times a day during every break & quiet moment away from studying, working, or cleaning."

"The danger is that these companies run spy software in the background, gathering all descriptions of personal data they can use to analyze their users and predict their behaviors. They then package and sell this data in the form of advertising placements."

"Social media has learned how to make their news feed scroll and notification addictive by hijacking human desires to regularly contact 'friends' and be aware of dangerous news. Many people are seriously addicted, spending twenty to fifty hours a week on social media. Quitting is almost impossible because all their friends are online."

"Stop yawning for a minute. I am getting to the end."

"All of this would be manageable if we could contain the effects of this private screen time inside a little box after school and work. But the psychological impact of the internet is attaching itself to every aspect of our lives. Social media helps destroy our ability to be amazing humans capable of high achievement and art."

"A distracted mind cannot see the world clearly, split between dozens of entertaining stories and to-do lists. Social media users look at the most difficult, rare, and beautiful situations and resolve to copy them even if the efforts do not justify the rewards. They can't enjoy the simple things around them because they are in a hurry to get to that "better life" that seems magical and unreal[cxxxv]."

"The social media user who spends far too much time passively watching videos, playing solo games, and trying to become rich, often loses much of his verbal and social skills."

"Digital citizens may be perceived as aloof, arrogant, talkative, or robotic by observers. They don't know how to read body language or hear tonality to connect with strangers. Online and offline relationships can become tedious and superficial because they don't resemble the fantasy lifestyle we want, nor do they seem real and genuine[cxxxvi]."

"This isolation and disconnection from real humans cannot be satisfied with small talk at work & parties, and this lonely individual may be in turmoil, blaming himself for lack of success with other people."

"That can be the cost of spending too much time in front of a screen and not enough time developing relationships with people. Do not discount what I am saying. The essence of a human is the type of relationship he or she has with others. If social media tricks users into trading real connections for the dopamine hits of 'likes' and meaningless messages, that is simply an awful thing to witness."

"One more thing. Never let the negativity of the world put you on the floor. Yes, we discussed immorality and dishonesty and most people are prone to weaknesses, but I truly believe that the average person does far more good than bad in his life. Manipulative forces are trying to turn us angry and mean because they want to pull our puppet strings to accumulate wealth and power. We must hunt for golden rays in the world to feed our light wolf, and ignore most news & gossip to starve our dark wolf."

Will yawned again. He couldn't stay awake, but he also couldn't fall asleep.

"Well, I think we have completed the last lesson for now. These lectures are nearly enough, there is so much more to say, yet it's time you get some rest. Good night, Will."

"Ahh, you mean that's it? Won't I see you anymore? No more hallucinations? No future interruptions?" Will asked.

"For now, yes."

"Are you coming back?" Will asked.

"I don't know. But believe this. I am always with you, even if you can't see me or hear me. When you get that intuitive feeling of what to do, know that it is your conscious guiding you like a guardian angel, giving you a path forward when nothing is certain."

"Goodbye, Will." Morgan got off the sofa and walked to the door. As he pulled on the handle, Will remembered his manners.

"Hey, Morgan," Will called out while still sitting slumped in his chair. "Thanks for everything. It's been a trip."

"It sure has."

RULE OF PRINCIPLE 48: *When confronted by Evil, most run away and try to pretend it is someone else's problem. Blinded by the allure of Evil's power and strength, some victims are ensnared by its tentacles, unable to escape. They pull others in their orbit into their hell. If you possess some wisdom & awareness, can you be an average person of principle who can walk up to Evil, stare it right in the eye & declare?: "F*ck off; I will not join you, not me, not today!"*

74. Night 26 - CRISIS

Will woke up suddenly in a daze. He had fallen asleep on the sofa in front of the television, still running political news. What time was it? Just after ten at night. Something in his gut was telling him something was seriously wrong.

He got up off the sofa and stumbled towards the bathroom. A vile wad of spit had accumulated in his mouth, and he had to spit it out before he gagged.

As Will ran the faucets to splash his face with some lukewarm water, he looked in the mirror. "God, I need a shave," he thought. "Angel, I should text her! See if she is all right."

The phone buzzed from a text message. Angel surprised him with an impromptu visit and was outside his apartment, waiting for him.

Will threw on his heavy winter coat, feeling a hefty bulge in the coat pocket. As he ran down the stairs to get to the apartment lobby, he felt the unbalanced feeling of vertigo. The walls were spinning, and it felt like he was climbing rather than descending.

He saw a strange man covered in black & tattoos get out of Angel's black SUV. The man was yelling and gesturing uncontrollably. Something about stealing his girlfriend? Will did not understand.

The man retreated to the car, reached in, and picked up a wooden baseball bat. Did he say he was going to bash Will's brains in? He approached menacingly with the bat down on his right side. What was he saying? What was going on here?

Angel was also screaming and yelling something Will couldn't understand. She was pleading with this attacker to stop, stomping her feet—a look of terror on her porcelain features.

Those muscular arms swung the bat hard, and it cut through nothing but air. It was not Will's quick reflexes. This man was so angry that he could not even aim straight. He swung again. Will now saw stars and stripes blanketing the night sky. Was he going to perish saluting to old glory? The ringing of his ears was deafening. It blocked out all other sounds, even the heaviness of his breath.

As he stumbled and fell on his bottom, his chest tightened like a snare drum. His heart was pumping so fast, yet he felt like gasping for air. His palm landed on the bulge in his coat pocket, and instinctively, he pulled out the Glock.

Crack! Crack! Crack! Now he could hear again. What did he do? He had shot indiscriminately into the air. Angel was screaming in shock.

Blackish red patches appeared on the man's chest through his white sports jersey. Despite Will's terrible aim, one shot had found its target. The man looked shocked as he realized how quickly the table had turned. He collapsed to his knees. So much black blood. Wasn't blood supposed to be bright red?

The look on the man's face was a mixture of fury and confusion. His eyes became sad and wide open as he realized his last three seconds on earth were up. He keeled over onto his stomach, his face buried in the snow.

Will also collapsed in the snow, not from labored breathing or the violence imposed on him, but from emotional shock. All the drops of red faded to blackness. Nothingness. Peace.

75. DAY 27 - RECOVERY

Ivy drip. White curtains and walls. Clean, cool bed sheets. Will found himself alone in a hospital bed at eleven the next morning. The exhausted, achy, numbed out feeling that he had been suffering from was finally gone. There was an elderly patient asleep in the next bed. His back turned to Will's bed.

He pressed the intercom, and a Latin-American nurse in blue scrubs appeared. Will asked the nurse why he had awakened in a gown in the hospital.

"Ah, you collapsed from exhaustion in front of your building, and EMT brought you here to recover. We gave you some sedatives and let you rest. You are scheduled for release tomorrow, pending some additional tests, because we can't find any medical issues with you."

"Is my girlfriend, Angel, here? She's a blonde woman in her twenties. He described her when the nurse looked confused.

"No one like that is here. Your parents are in the visitors' waiting area. Would you like to speak to the attending physician on call?'

Will nodded yes. For the first time in weeks, he felt refreshed and rejuvenated. Like a new man ready to start a new chapter of his life. Then he remembered.

The body. The blood. Will remembered he had killed someone. A stranger. Right in front of Angel.

His mind flooded with worry as he thought about the impending consequences. Were the authorities going to arrest him? How long would he go to jail? What would his friends and family think? Would he lose his career? His girlfriend? His reputation?

A man in a white lab coat briskly walked into the room, disturbing his thoughts. His physician looked to be in his early thirties, Eastern European or maybe Egyptian; he could not tell.

"Well, Mr. Evans. Good to see you are awake. How are you feeling?" The doctor stood in front of his bed and picked up the hospital chart for Will.

"Fine. Can you tell me what happened? How did I get here?"

Frowning, the doctor read the rest of the intake forms and said, "EMT wrote that you were found in the snow by your neighbor, Mrs. Hoffman, just outside your apartment door. No bruises, cuts, concussions. No heart conditions, no medical issues. It looks like you collapsed from exhaustion and some traces of marijuana in your system."

"Are the police going to arrest me?" Will asked.

"For what?" the doctor asked in surprise. "I don't see any police arrest warrants on your file."

"I do have to ask one more question. Why were three shots fired from your gun? Police officers found a handgun near you when you collapsed and some bullets discharged from the chamber. I have to ask just to complete your medical history, so there are no future problems," the doctor said apologetically.

Will quickly calculated in his head. The doctor did not mention a crime scene so far. He did not see a police officer waiting outside or any indication anyone was going to arrest him. This was no time for honesty.

"What? No. I did not shoot anyone. There was a noise, and it spooked me. And I certainly am not suicidal, if that is what you think." Will stated indignantly.

"That is good to hear. We will run some additional simple blood tests and keep you overnight for observation. Pending a clean bill of health, we can have you out of here early tomorrow morning. I will let your parents know about your condition, and they can visit you soon, okay?"

"Yes, thank you, Dr. ….?" He did know his name.

"Dr. Kholonsov. Good luck." The physician was already halfway out the door. Just one of the dozens of patients to see throughout his shift. Nothing worth spending time on, now that he was clearing Will of any medical matters.

Will talked to his parents and confirmed his suspicions. He casually asked if they discovered anything new in the news.

Nothing unusual. No one other than the hospital nurses had contacted them about his emergency admission. He had hallucinated the whole thing, just like his conversations with Morgan.

76. RESOLUTION

It's been a week since Will's episode. The sleepless nights are gone, and with it, Morgan's visits. Angel is sitting at one of those fancy boutique coffee shops sipping a latte. She looks freshly scrubbed, fashionably dressed in a white sweater and trousers—a lavender hint in the air.

Will orders a cappuccino and greets her with a peck on the cheek.

"Hi, Sweetie, you are looking well."

"Hi, Angel. Girl, you look amazing, all in white."

Awkward silence. Then both started talking at once.

"Will, I…" "Can I?...." They both giggled at the uncomfortable conversation.

"It was a little disappointing when you did not come to the hospital," he said.

Angel excused herself, "I stopped by late, but the receptionist prevented me from seeing you. Visiting hours had just ended."

"And after that?" he questioned her.

"I was a little afraid to see you. You were acting all sorts of weird, even for you. But then I heard from your parents that you had not slept in weeks and were kind of exhausted and delusional," she said.

She continued. "First, I wanted to try dating you again. Then I wanted to break up. After our last date, the texts got a little strange, kind of needy. It's been a couple of weeks since then, and everything has changed again."

"Angel, I have cleaned up my act. The weed is gone. No more drinking. Okay, less drinking. I am going to quit my job and accept another offer from a better firm. The hospitalization was a wake-up call, and I am taking this seriously."

"That is so good to hear. But please don't be too serious. I like it when it gets crazy," Angel said.

Will agreed, "No worries…..Um, was this all just a fling, a rebound for old time sake, or did you want to try again?"

"Will, I have dated many, many guys." She paused.

"And?" he waited for the door to be slammed shut.

"You are the only guy I have met to be the right combination of what I want and what I need. My partying with rich jerks and bad boys is over," she said.

Will's heart leaped forward." Yes! Um, I agree with you. I'd love to give it another go."

"Will, I am late."

"Late for what?" Will asked.

"You know, late," Angel confirmed.

"Oh, my God. You mean…?," he gasped.

"Yep, you are going to be a daddy."

FINAL THOUGHTS

**If you self-identify yourself as a conservative with traditional values, it is highly probable that you will find much of the material highly offensive.

This guide is not an attack on any particular group or industry but their immoral behavior and the consequences of that dishonesty. I acknowledge a substantial number of educated readers have difficulty separating the two and might view criticism of these industries, nations, or religions as a personal attack. I profoundly apologize should you feel this way.

Many anti-establishment liberals may enjoy the ferocity with which I ravage through many industries and socio-economic groups that frankly deserve it. They may, or may not, appreciate my advocacy for small businesses, criminal justice reform, government regulation, and organized religion rather than anarchy & atheism .

The readers that would appreciate this writing the most are those who can set aside their personal beliefs and understand that what may be suitable for them may be inappropriate for others. For example, many chapters require readers to hold two competing ideas in their head and accept both as valid.

I realize that asking atheists and socialists to think about the benefits of weekly spiritual gatherings is a tough sell. Am I advising Liberals and Conservatives to put aside their differences and compromise? Yes! Instructing union & low wage workers to consider starting their own business is also likely to be met with resistance. Very few are that flexible in their beliefs.

Chasing this small percentage of the population on a topic like ethics and morality will probably get me into a whole heap of trouble, but unexpressed thoughts inscribe deathbed regrets. Some things need to be said, and someone has to report them. With reckless abandon, we leap into the future. 'Consequences be damned.'

Most of the new theories in this book are the synthetic combinations of popular psychology and academic research with recent newsworthy stories of impropriety and criminality.

New philosophical ideation without extensive research or verification is vulnerable to attack by critics. That is fair. But that leads to a new question: How does one validate morality concepts without being influenced by subconscious personal biases taught by parental and societal influences?

I don't have an answer to that dilemma. If any reader comes across research that supports or disproves any theory in this book, their input is welcome.

I can't entirely agree with scholars' notions that academic experts should screen all personal psychology and values philosophies before releasing approved schoolings into the public sphere. Billions are living lives full of false narratives and disempowering beliefs. In the absence of rational coherent thought, we tend to accept emotional-based intuition free of logical principles. Every writer and speaker who can educate positive alternative realities contribute to world peace and spiritual growth in their unique way.

I believe that designing universal held principles of moral values and codes of conduct applicable to most cultures requires brainstorming, ideation, discussion, and flexibility. To solve global poverty, growing pollution, widespread crime, and mental illnesses requires that we all speak a common language of values and beliefs. When we do what is right instead of what we fear, we can move forward.

While I am willing to accept that some 'means' ideas may be flawed or disproven, I stand firm by my moral code, the forty-eight rules. I believe them to be logical and rational based on seventeen years of formal education and over three thousand books, on a wide variety of subjects, consumed over four decades of life.

Quite a few of my ideas are 'means' and not 'ends' to understanding why so many are behaving so immorally. I have expressed views to fill in the gaps like 'vehicles ' so that non-academics can connect the psychological causes of unethical behavior to my moderate-liberal rules of conduct. My contribution is putting forward some new ideas of how the world works, and perhaps others can build on and expand these theories. Or take it in a completely different direction. It is not up to me how the wind blows.

ABOUT THE AUTHOR

James S. Zakaria is the author of Rebel, Untethered; Masterminds Are The Key; 48 Rules For Raging Against The World; and The Cry Of Bright Shadows. James lives in Toronto and assists entrepreneurs & other organizations with writing growth-oriented Business Plan Summaries. Please communicate with the author via email: JamesZakaria7@gmail.com

END NOTES:

---

i. M. Scott Peck, 1978, The Road Less Traveled, Pg 45, Simon & Schuster, New York.

ii. Greene, Robert, 2018, The Laws of Nature, Introduction, Viking Publishing, New York

iii. Stutz, Phil, & Barry Michaels, 2012, The Tools, pg 133, Random House, New York

iv. Deepak Chopra, Debbie Ford, & Marianne Williamson, 2010, The Shadow Effect, Pg 9, Harper One, New York

v. https://crossingenres.com/you-know-that-charming-story-about-the-two-wolves-its-a-lie-d0d93ea4ebff

vi. Barbara Colorso, 2005, Just Because It's Not Wrong, Doesn't Make It Right, Pg 33, Penguin Canada,

vii. Deepak Chopra, Debbie Ford, Marianne Wiliamson, 2010, The Shadow Effect, Pg 2 & 10, HarperOne, NY.

viii. Deepak Chopra, Debbie Ford, & Marianne Williamson, 2010, The Shadow Effect, Pg 12, Harper One, New York

ix. Deepak Chopra, Debbie Ford, Marianne Wiliamson, 2010, The Shadow Effect, Pg 169, HarperOne, NY.

x. Jordan B. Person, 2018, 12 Rules For Life, Pg 16, Random House, Toronto

xi. Jordan B. Person, 2018, 12 Rules For Life, Pg 17, Random House, Toronto

xii. Gabor Mate, 1999, Scattered Minds, Introduction, Random House, Toronto

xiii. https://www.antislavery.org/slavery-today/modern-slavery/

xiv. Clason, George, 1926, The Richest Man In Babylon, Pg 16, Signet Publishing, New York

xv. https://www.scientificamerican.com/article/do-prisons-make-us-safer/

xvi. https://www.npr.org/2015/07/06/418585084/the-new-science-behind-our-unfair-criminal-justice-system

xvii. https://www.nytimes.com/2018/11/14/us/prison-reform-bill-republicans-democrats.html

xviii. https://www.theguardian.com/law/2011/apr/11/judges-lenient-break

xix. https://bulletin.represent.us/happens-prisons-privatize-john-oliver-arms/ Last Week Tonight With John Oliver, HBO,

xx. Arianna Huffington, 2010, Third World America, Pg 6, Crown Publishing, New York

xxi. Arianna Huffington, 2010, Third World America, Pg 11, Crown Publishing, New York

xxii. Barbara Coloroso, 2005, Just Because It's Not Wrong Doesn't Make It Right, pg 30, Penguin Pub, NY

xxiii. Deepak Chopra, Debbie Ford, Marianne Wiliamson, 2010, The Shadow Effect, Pg 114, HarperOne, NY

xxiv. Coloros, Barbara, 2005, Just Because It's Not Wrong Doesn't Make It Right, pg 22, New York, Penguin Pub

xxv. Ian Leslie, 2011, Born Liars, Anansi Press, Toronto

xxvi. https://en.wikipedia.org/wiki/Greed

xxvii. M. Scott Peck, 1978, The Road Less Traveled, Pg 24, Simon & Schuster, New York

xxviii. M. Scott Peck, 1978, The Road Less Traveled, Pg 38, Simon & Schuster, New York

xxix. Mark Manson, 2016, The Subtle Art Of Not Giving A F*ck, Pg 206, 210, HarperOne, NY

xxx. https://marisapeer.com/i-am-enough-marisa-peer/

xxxi. Jonice Webb, 2014, Running On Empty, Pg 14, Pg 19, Morgan James Publishing, New York

xxxii. Deepak Chopra, Debbie Ford, Marianne Williamson, 2010, The Shadow Effect, Pg 89-90, HarperOne, NY

xxxiii. Deepak Chopra, Debbie Ford, Marianne Wiliamson, 2010, The Shadow Effect, Pg 16, HarperOne, NY.

xxxiv. Deepak Chopra, Debbie Ford, Marianne Wiliamson, 2010, The Shadow Effect, Pg 35, HarperOne, NY.

xxxv. Robert Greene, 2018, The Laws of Human Nature, Pg 52, Viking Publishing, New York

xxxvi. Jordan B. Person, 2018, 12 Rules For Life, Pg 23, Random House, Toronto

xxxvii. https://torontolife.com/city/the-great-burnout-recession-survivors-didnt-count-on-the-surge-in-workload-the-smaller-paycheque-and-the-all-consuming-resentment-a-story-about-workplace-in-hell-with-no-escape/

xxxviii. Barbara Ehrenreich, 2009, Bright-Sided, Pg 174, 178, Metropolitan Books, New York

xxxix. Phil Stutz & Barry Michels, 2012, The Tools, Pg 106, Spiegel & Grau, New York

xl.   Barabara Coloroso, 2005, Just Because It's Not Wrong Doesn't Make It Right, Pg 29, Penguin Books, Toronto

xli.   Gabor Mate, 1999, Scattered Minds, Pg 297-300, Vintage Canada, Toronto

xlii.   Don Miguel Ruiz, 1997, The Four Agreements, pg 5, Amber-Allen Publishing, USA

xliii. Don Miguel Ruiz, 1997, The Four Agreements, pg 15, Amber-Allen Publishing, USA

xliv.   https://www.theguardian.com/commentisfree/cifamerica/2009/jul/23/newspapers-internet-adverstising

xlv.   Don Miguel, Ruiz, 1997, The Four Agreements, pg 18, Amber-Allen Publishing, California

xlvi.   Don Miguel, Ruiz, 1997, The Four Agreements, Pg 7, Amber-Allen Publishing, California

xlvii. Barbara Coloroso, 2010, Just Because It's Not Wrong Doesn't Make It Right, Pg 169, Penguin Canada, Toronto

xlviii. Brene Brown, 2010, The Gifts Of Imperfection, pg 42, Hazelden, Minnesota

xlix.   Mark Manson, 2016, The Subtle Art Of Not Giving A F*ck, Pg 15, HarperOne, New York

l.   Arianna Huffington, 2010, Third World America, Pg 197, Crown Publishing, NY

li.   Deepak Chopra, Debbie Ford, Marianne Williamson, 2010, The Shadow Effect, Pg 23, HarperOne, NY

lii.   Ian Leslie, 2011, Born Liars, Pg 68, House of Anansi Press, Toronto

liii.   Jonice Webb with Christine Musello, 2014, Running on Empty, Pg 99, Morgan James, New York

liv.   https://www.usatoday.com/story/life/people/2018/02/20/how-common-sexual-misconduct-hollywood/1083964001

lv.   Jordan B. Peterson, 2018, 12 Rules For Life, Pg 83, Random House, Toronto

lvi.   Mark Manson, 2016, The Subtle Art Of Not Giving A F*ck, Pg 9,13, Harper One, New York

lvii.   https://www.theatlantic.com/health/archive/2016/01/when-are-you-really-an-adult/422487/

lviii. Jordan B. Peterson, 2018, 12 Rules For Life, Pg 4, Random House, Toronto

lix.   Don Mguel Ruiz, 1997, The Four Agreements, Pg 96, Amber-Allen Publishing, USA

lx.   Don Miguel Ruiz, 1997 The Four Agreements, pg 22, Amber-Allen Publishing, USA

lxi.   https://ourworldindata.org/terrorism

lxii.   M. Scott Peck, 1978, The Road Less Traveled, Pg 23, Simon & Schuster, New York

lxiii. M. Scott Peck, 1978, The Road Less Traveled, Pg 45, Simon & Schuster, New York

lxiv.   Coloros, Barbara, 2005, Just Because It's Not Wrong Doesn't Make It Right, pg 1, Penguin Publishing, New York,

lxv.   Deepak Chopra, Debbie Ford, Marianne Wiliamson, 2010, The Shadow Effect, Pg 86, HarperOne, NY

lxvi.   Malcolm Gladwell, 2002, The Tipping Point, Pg 142, BackBay Books, New York

lxvii. Sue Palmer, 2006, Toxic Childhood Pg 25-26, Orion Paperback, London, UK

lxviii. Sue Palmer, 2006, Toxic Childhood Pg 23, Orion Paperback, London, UK

lxix.   Sue Palmer, 2006, Toxic Childhood Pg 26-31, Orion Paperback, London, UK

lxx.   Ian leslie, 2011, Born Liars, Pg 46, Anansi Press, London

lxxi.   Phil Stutz & Barry Michels, 2012, The Tools, Pg 187-189, Spiegel & Grau, New York

lxxii. https://www.npr.org/sections/goatsandsoda/2018/04/20/60416 9277/a-debt-crisis-seems-to-have-come-out-of-nowhere

lxxiii. https://www.newyorker.com/magazine/2019/09/30/is-meritocracy-making-everyone-miserable

lxxiv. Michael Sandler, 2020, The Tyranny of Merit, Introduction, Farrar, Straus and Giroux, NY

lxxv.   Leonard Sax, 2016, The Collapse of Parenting, Pg 10, Basic Books, New York

lxxvi. Augusten Burroughs, 2012, This is How, Pg 57, St Martin's Press, New York

lxxvii. Leonard Sax, 2016, The Collapse of Parenting, Pg 18, Basic Books, New York

lxxviii. Leonard Sax, 2016, The Collapse of Parenting, Pg 14, Basic Books, New York

lxxix. https://www.theguardian.com/money/2013/feb/13/banks-accused-misleading-investment-advice-fsa

lxxx.   Leonard Sax, 2016, The Collapse of Parenting, Pg 19, Basic Books, New York

lxxxi. Dave Ramsey, 2003, Financial Peace Revisited, Pg 7-9, Viking Penguin Press, New York

lxxxii.   Barbara Ehrenreich, 2009, Bright Sided, Pg 108-109, Metropolitan Books, New York

lxxxiii.   Susan Jacoby, 2009, The Age of American Unreason, Pg 244, Random House, New York

lxxxiv.   Mark Manson, 2016, The Subtle Art Of Not Giving A F*ck, Pg 73, HarperOne, New York

lxxxv.   https://www.cnn.com/2012/09/04/opinion/brazile-unions/index.html

lxxxvi.   https://www.nytimes.com/2008/04/16/us/16labor.html

lxxxvii.   https://securityintelligence.com/articles/10-myths-and-misconceptions-about-industrial-espionage/

lxxxviii. Robert Greene, 2018, The Laws of Human Nature, Pg 576, Viking Publishing, New York

lxxxix.   Barbara Ehrenreich, 2009, Bright-Sided, Pg 55, Metropolitan Books, New York

xc.   Deepak Chopra, Debbie Ford, Marianne Wiliamson, 2010, The Shadow Effect, Pg 12, HarperOne, NY.

xci.   Arielly, Dan, PREDICTABLY IRRATIONAL , Pg 18

xcii.   Robert Fulghum, 2004, All I Really Needed To Know I Learned In Kindergarten, Intro, Ballantine Books, New York

xciii.   Phil Stutz & Barry Michels, 2012 The Tools, Pg 35, Spiegel & Grau, New York

xciv.   Deepak Chopra, Debbie Ford, Marianne Wiliamson, 2010, The Shadow Effect, Pg 35, HarperOne, NY.

xcv.   Deepak Chopra, Debbie Ford, Marianne Wiliamson, 2010, The Shadow Effect, Pg 87, HarperOne, NY.

xcvi.   Tony Robbins, 2017, Unshakeable, Pg 47-49, Simon & Schuster, New York

xcvii.   Phil Stutz & Barry Michels, 2012, The Tools, Pg 130, Spiegel & Grau, New York

xcviii.   Deepak Chopra, Debbie Ford, Marianne Wiliamson, 2010, The Shadow Effect, Pg 14, HarperOne, NY

xcix.   https://www.cleveland.com/business/2016/01/why_do_70_percent_of_lottery_w.html

c.   https://www.psychologytoday.com/ca/blog/mind-in-the-machine/201612/fear-and-anxiety-drive-conservatives-political-attitudes

ci.   Malcolm Gladwell, 2005, Blink, Pg 91, Hachette Book Group, New York

cii.   Manson, Mark, 2019, Everything is F*cked, HarperOne, New York ciii. Arianna Huffington, 2010, Third World America, Pg 129-130, Crown Publishing, New York

civ. Seth Godin, 2011, Poke The Box, Pg 70, Domino Publishing, USA

cv. Ken Robinson, 2009, The Element: How Finding Your Passion Changes Everything, Penguin Books, New York

cvi. Barabara Coloroso, 2005, Just Because It's Not Wrong Doesn't Make It Right, Pg 25, Penguin Books, Toronto

cvii. Barbara Coloroso, 2010, Just Because It's Not Wrong Doesn't Make It Right, Pg 43, Penguin Canada, Toronto

cviii. Deepak Chopra, Debbie Ford, Marianne Wiliamson, 2010, The Shadow Effect, Pg 86, HarperOne, NY.

cix. Gabor Mate, 1999, Scattered Minds, Pg 15, Random House, Toronto

cx. https://www.ted.com/talks/sir_ken_robinson_do_schools_kill_creativity?language=en#t-1686

cxi. Barbara Coloroso, 2005, Just Because It's Not Wrong, Does Not Make It Right, Pg 205, Penguin Canada, Toronto

cxii. https://www.cnn.com/2020/10/21/business/purdue-pharma-guilty-plea/index.html

cxiii. https://time.com/longform/portugal-drug-use-decriminalization/

cxiv. http://www.oprah.com/spirit/confessions-of-a-shoplifter-reasons-people-steal/all

cxv. Coloros, Barbara, 2005, Just Because It's Not Wrong Doesn't Make It Right, pg 30,, Penguin Publishing, NY

cxvi. https://www.psychologytoday.com/ca/blog/what-the-wild-things-are/201107/gains-and-losses-helping-people-stop-stealing

cxvii. https://en.wikipedia.org/wiki/Bad_apples#

cxviii. Bakan, Joel, 2004, The Corporation, pg 79, Penguin Canada, Toronto

cxix. Phil Stutz & Barry Michels, 2012, The Tools, Pg 106, Spiegel & Grau, New York

cxx. Deepak Chopra, Debbie Ford, Marianne Williamson, 2010, The Shadow Effect, Pg 105, HarperOne, NY

cxxi. Neil Pasricha, 2016, The Happiness Equation, Pg 15, Putnam Publishing, NY

cxxii. M. Scott Peck, 1978, The Road Less Traveled, Pg 26, Simon & Schuster, New York

cxxiii. https://en.wikipedia.org/wiki/Terrorism

cxxiv. https://www.cnbc.com/2019/09/17/uber-drivers-are-protesting-again-heres-what-the-job-is-really-like.html

cxxv. Eric Baker, 2018, Barking Up The Wrong Tree, Pg 30, HarperOne, NY

cxxvi. M. Scott Peck, 1979, The Road Less Travelled, Pg 71, Simon & Schuster, New York

cxxvii. Jordan Peterson, 2018, 12 Rules For Life, Pg 130, Random House, Toronto

cxxviii. Phil Stutz & Barry Michels, 2012, The Tools, Pg 186, Spiegel & Grau, New York

cxxix. Gabor Mate,1999, Scattered Minds, Pg 101, Vintage Canada, Toronto

cxxx. Phil Stutz & Barry Michels, 2012, The Tools, Pg 130, Spiegel & Grau, New York

cxxxi. Jordan Peterson, 2018, 12 Rules For Life, Pg 120, Random House, Toronto

cxxxii. Phil Stutz & Barry Michels, 2012, The Tools, Pg 109, Spiegel & Grau, New York

cxxxiii. https://www.thechicagoschool.edu/insight/from-the-magazine/a-virtual-life/

cxxxiv. https://time.com/4457110/internet-trolls/

cxxxv. Leonard Sax, 2016, The Collapse Of Parenting, Pg 90, 108, Basic Books, NY

cxxxvi. Gary John Bishop, 2016, Unfu*k Yourself, Pg 60, HarperOne, New York